D0851849

Introductory Hebrew
Grammar

Introductory Hebrew Grammar

by

R. Laird Harris, Ph.D.

WM. B. EERDMANS PUBLISHING COMPANY

Grand Rapids   Michigan

Fourth edition, September 1955

Tenth printing, June 1979

ISBN 0-8028-1100-0

PHOTOLITHOPRINTED BY CUSHING - MALLOY, INC.
ANN ARBOR, MICHIGAN, UNITED STATES OF AMERICA

To

MY PARENTS

Preface

The Hebrew Grammar presented herewith has been used by the author for some eleven years of teaching the language to mature students with no Hebrew background. First hectographed, then mimeographed several times, it is now presented in more permanent form having been Vari-typed then printed by the photo-offset process. The preparation of this second edition re-photographed from the original material has given an opportunity to correct the typographical mistakes of the earlier printing without (it is hoped) introducing many new ones.

The Grammar introduces some departures from the usual presentations. One feature helpful to the beginner is the notice in the vocabularies of Biblical names and expressions where these may be helpful in memorizing the utterly strange vocables. The vocabulary words themselves have been chosen in accordance with the word frequency lists of Harper and with the use of other materials.

The exercises were made with the beginner in mind. The early sentences are not from the Bible on the principle that a primer should not consist of excerpts from Shakespeare and Emerson. The sentences are short, partly to encourage the student and also to build up eye span and phrase comprehension. The sentences for the most part use every vocabulary word at least twice and exhibit about all of the points of grammar taken up. They thus show in compact form (only equal to about a dozen pages of Biblical text) all of the Bible's important words and most of its grammatical principles. In the exercises of the first edition, varieties of pointing, e.g. compensatory heightening and implicit doubling, were exhibited without close regard to Biblical usage of particular words. In deference to criticism that this taught bad Hebrew, these normalizations have been largely corrected in this edition.

Another detail has proved helpful in teaching, though it is confessed it will at first confuse teachers. The persons of the verb paradigm have been reversed from the time-honored Semitic order of third, second, and first. The reason was that students were found persistently calling third persons first simply because in all their other language study the first person headed the paradigm. It seemed easier to turn the paradigm around than to reverse every student. Results seem very much to justify the experiment and advanced students seem to have no difficulty in going on to other grammars and to the study of different Semitic languages. Note also the unusual use of כָּתַב in the paradigm on p. 75 rather than קָטַל so as to show the occurrences of Dagesh Lene. This is a student suggestion, though Gesenius mentions the need (p. 116, note).

A word of explanation about the handling of accents may be given to those used to other methods of teaching. It will be noted at once that the verb is presented with rules governing the important vowels and their changes, while rules for accent are presented only late in the book. The usual method of presenting accent rules first is exemplified in one beginners' grammar which gives on p. 8 eleven uses of the Metheg before any Hebrew words are given to practice accents with! The difficulty with emphasizing the accents as a means of learning word forms is threefold. First the accents in the Masoretic text are not the original accents of the Hebrew Bible. The history of the accent shift is unclear, but the present accents are somewhat artificial indicating synagogue intonation as well as true accent.

Second, the changes occasioned by accent can not always be understood without knowing the ground form of the word in question. Thus the Niphal pf. of the Ayin-Waw verb has a qames in the preformative syllable lengthened from an original pathah. But the Hiphil of these verbs in this syllable has a sere lengthened not from the original pathah, but from the later hiriq. Rather than explain every ground form (some of which are debatable), it seems simpler just to tell the beginner that the verbs have certain vowels in certain places regardless of what accent shifts occurred. Later study of both ground forms and accents is, of course, expected.

Thirdly, accent effects are not invariable and can not be counted upon. The minor pauses, like zaqeph qaton sometimes cause vowel lengthening; sometimes they do not. Sentence rhythm in the phenomenon of nasog 'ahor sometimes operates; Bergstrasser's "Hebraische Grammatik" (p. 130) remarks there are 3500 places where it might operate and does not. The student can observe these changes, but can not predict them.

It would not help, however, just to memorize the verb by rote without regard to accent, for there are many minor variations which would hopelessly confuse a student who just learned the regular verb and five principle irregular types.

For these reasons the present system uses rules to indicate the principal vowels or landmarks in verb forms. Vowels which frequently vary for any reason are minimized as not essential for a beginner to know in order to get to reading Hebrew. It may be added however, that teachers who feel the need to do so can introduce Lesson 15 on accents immediately after Lesson 5 as it does not build to any extent on the intervening material.

The system presented herewith has had some success. The author learned it and the importance of stressing the verb from his former teacher and present chief, Dr. Allan A. MacRae to whom hearty thanks and significant credit are given. It is of course expected that this book and this method will be regarded as an introduction only and that the student will later pursue all subjects of the grammar further in a standard work such as Gesenius-Kautzsch-Cowley, 2nd Eng.ed. References are frequently made to this work as well as occasionally to Bergstrasser's "Hebraische Grammatik."

Fortunately, the student is now better off with regard to lexicons than the text (p.47) indicates. Recently the edition of Gesenius by F. Buhl has been reprinted abroad (Springer-Verlag, Berlin,Gottingen, Heidelberg) and there is appearing - soon to be finished- the excellent new lexicon of Koehler and Baumgartner, "Dictionary of the Hebrew and Aramaic Old Testament in English and German" published in this country by Eerdmans, publishers of this Grammar.

It is a pleasure to repeat in this edition the author's thanks to many: to Dr. MacRae, mentioned above, his teacher, friend, and President of Faith Theological Seminary where the author has learned much while teaching; to his instructor in more advanced Hebrew, Dr. E.A.Speiser of the University of Pennsylvania, the excellence of whose Hebrew teaching is not at all evidenced by this little presentation; and above all to his many patient students who have persisted through the years in spite of laryngeals, dageshes, etc. He only hopes that their effort and his instruction may prove useful in their task of faithfully interpreting the written Word of God to our needy generation.

Table of Contents

Introductory Hebrew Grammar

INTRODUCTORY HEBREW GRAMMAR

Lesson 1   The Alphabet

As mentioned in the Introduction, ancient Hebrew wrote only the consonants. The alphabet used by the Biblical authors consisted of 22 letters which parallel in general the letters of our English alphabet. Indeed the alphabet was invented, it seems, by Semites in or near Palestine shortly after 1800 B.C. (cf. Albright, BASOR, Apr. 1948, p.12). It was carried by the Phoenicians to the Greeks at about 1000 or 700 B.C. and thence descended to us through the Romans. The Hebrews wrote for centuries using only consonants, but in the early pre-Christian and post-Biblical times when the Jews began speaking the Aramaic more than Hebrew, there was felt a need for the marking of certain of the long vowels. At this time a few of the so-called vowel letters or *matres lectionis* were added. This system of vowel indication was only a makeshift, however, and in the early Middle Ages vowel markings or pointings were invented by a school of Jewish scholars called Masoretes. As the consonantal text was by that time standardized and was very scrupulously regarded, these vowel points were placed below or above the consonants they followed. The system of pointing in use today is called the Tiberian after the Jewish community which invented it. Two other systems are known, called the Babylonian and Palestinian, but these are not important. It may be observed that the present Hebrew text has behind it three stages of writing - first the consonantal text, then the consonants with vowel letters marking some of the long vowels, then the consonants with vowel letters and complete vowel points. In this lesson only some of the consonants will be used - those which sound like their English equivalents - and some of the vowel points. The letters can best be memorized by practice with words.

The Consonants

Print	Writing	Translit.	Name	English Equivalent
בּ	בּ	b	Beth	With dot, hard like b
כ	כ	b̲		Without dot, soft - v
גּ	גּ	g	Gimel	With dot like hard g
ג	ג	g̲		Without dot, similar but breath not completely stopped
דּ	דּ	d	Daleth	With dot, hard like d
ד	ד	d̲		Like th in "this"
ה	ה	h	He (hay)	Like h. Silent after vowels.

Print	Writing	Translit.	Name	English Equivalent Sound
ו	ו	w	Waw	Like w. Silent after vowels
ז	ז	z	Zayin	Like English z
ט	ט	ṭ	Teth	An emphatic t
כ	כ	k	Kaph	With dot like k
כ	כ	ḵ		Without dot about the same; breath not completely stopped
ך	ך			Form used at end of words
ל	ל	l	Lamedh	Like l
מ	מ	m	Mem	Like m
ם	ם			Form used at end of words
נ	נ	n	Nun	Like n
ן	ן			Form used at end of words
ס	ס	s	Samech	Like s
פ	פ	p	Pe	With dot like p
פ	פ	p̲	(Pay)	Without dot like f
ף	ף			Form used at end of words
ק	ק	q	Qoph	Like q in "racquet" – a deep k made against the soft palate
ר	ר	r	Resh	Like r
שׁ	שׁ	š	Shin	Like sh in "she"
ת	ת	t	Tau	With the dot like t
ת	ת	t̲		Without dot like th in "thin"

The Full Vowels (Shown written with Mem, מ)

Vowel	Translit.	Name	Pronunciation
מָ	ā	Qames	Long a as in "father"
מַ	a	Pathah	Short a as in "cat"
מִ or מִי	i or iy	Hiriq	With '(Yodh) usually long; without, may be long or short. When short, like i in "pin" When long, like i in "machine"
מֵ or מֵי	e or ey	Sere	The quality of e in "they." With '(Yodh) usually long; without, long or short in quantity.
מֶ	ɛ	Seghol	The quality of e in "met" but long or short in quantity
מֹ or מוֹ	ō or ōw	Holem	Like o in "hole." With ו (Waw) usually long; otherwise long or short as regards quantity
מוּ	ūw	Shureq	Like u in "brute," usually long
מֻ	u	Qibbus	The same as Shureq, but more usually short
מָ	o	Qames-Hatuph	Rather like the Qames and indistinguishable from it in sign This is short o; Qames is long a

The system of transliteration given above differs slightly from other standard systems, particularly in that its purpose is to represent in English characters as closely as practicable just what the Masoretes wrote down. In particular, the vowel letters are here represented by y or w which (as in the Hebrew equivalents) does not change the vowel pronunciation. The length of vowels is not marked in this system just as it is not marked, invariably, by the Masoretes. The sign for holem is not intended to imply that it is always a long vowel. Sometimes it is not. Rather it is just a convenient designation to distinguish it from Qames-Hatuph.

Classes of Vowels

The above vowels seem to have been derived ultimately from three main vowels, A, I, and U. The E-vowels go with the I class, and the O-vowels with the U-class. To the first class, the A-vowels, belong the Qames and Pathah always and the Hiriq and Seghol sometimes. To the second class, the I-vowels, belong the Hiriq, Sere, and Seghol. To the third class, the U-vowels, belong the Holem, Shureq, Qibbus, and Qames-Hatuph. Changes in accent and syllables frequently cause modification of the Hebrew vowels, but the changes will regularly cause modification from one vowel to another in the same class. A vowel does not turn into a heterogeneous vowel (one in a different class) except under special circumstances. These changes will be studied at length later.

Vocabulary (The names for practice, not memorization)

שֵׁת	šet	Seth	תֻּבַל	tubal	Tubal	זָכַר	zākar	he remembered
גָּד	gād	Gad	הֶבֶל	hebel	Abel	שָׁמַר	šāmar	he guarded
לוֹט	lōwt	Lot	דָּוִד	dāwid	David	פָּקַד	pāqad	he visited
דָּן	dān	Dan	שֵׁם	šem	Shem	סוּס	sūws	a horse
נוּן	nūwn	Nun	מֹשֶׁה	mōšeh	Moses	בֵּן	ben	a son

The Sentence

The sentence end or end of a Biblical verse is marked by the sign : A sentence with a finite verb usually has the verb at the beginning, the subject next, and the object last, thus "Moses guarded a horse" would be: שָׁמַר מֹשֶׁה סוּס A sentence without a finite verb, but having the copula "is" is usually expressed in Hebrew without any verb, thus: "Seth is a son" שֵׁת בֵּן:. These are called verbal and nominal sentences respectively.

Exercises

A. Translate and practice reading aloud until the letters are familiar:

1. זָכַר לוֹט בֶּן׃   2. שָׁמַר שֵׁת סוּס׃   3. פָּקַד מֹשֶׁה בֶּן׃

zākar lōwṭ ben   šāmar šeṯ suws   pāqad mōšɛh ben

4. דָּוִד׃   5. זָכַר הֶבֶל בֶּן׃   6. שָׁמַר נוּן בֶּן׃   7. שֵׁת בֶּן׃

dāwid   zākar hɛbɛl ben   šāmar nūwn ben   ben šeṯ

8. נוּן בֶּן׃   9. שָׁמַר תֻּבַל סוּס׃   10. שֵׁם בֶּן׃   11. דָּן בֶּן׃

ben nūwn   šāmar tubal suws   ben šem   dān ben

12. שָׁמַר׃   13. זָכַר דָּן בֶּן׃   14. גָּד בֶּן׃   15. פָּקַד נוּן בֶּן׃

šāmar   ben dān zākar   ben gāḏ   ben nūwn pāqad

B. Transliterate the following:

1. מֹשֶׁה׃   2. תֵּבֵל׃   3. דָּוִד׃   4. לוֹט׃   5. הֶבֶל׃   6. שֵׁם׃

7. שֵׁת׃   8. דָּן׃   9. נוּן׃   10. זָכַר דָּוִד׃   11. פָּקַד בֶּן׃

12. שֵׁם׃   13. שָׁמַר לוֹט בֶּן׃   14. שָׁמַר בֶּן סוּס׃   15. זָכַר

16. פָּקַד בֶּן׃   17. זָכַר הֶבֶל בֶּן׃   18. שֵׁת בֶּן׃   דָּוִד׃

C. Translate the following into Hebrew:
1. Seth is a son. 2. Gad remembered a son. 3. He guarded a horse. 4. Abel visited. 5. Nun. 6. Lot. 7. Moses remembered. 8. David is a son. 9. Tubal visited a son.

The Alphabet – continued

Several of the remaining letters of the Hebrew alphabet have peculiarities of pronunciation which may be made easier to understand by a consideration of the way the vocal organs operate in voice production.

Voice sounds may be divided, in general, into voiced and voiceless sounds. In the former, the vocal cords are buzzing; in the latter they are not. Thus b is voiced; p is not. English has three sounds which are made with the nasal passages open, m, n, and ng -all of which are voiced. There are, further, several sounds in which the vocal passage becomes completely closed, as b, p, d, g, k, q, and t. These are called stops. The corresponding sounds in which the stoppage is not complete may be called fricatives, such as v, f, th, etc. For instance, b is a voiced stop; f a voiceless fricative. The stops may be further classified – and frica-

atives too – by the place where the stoppage or friction
occurs. Thus the b and p are labial stops, formed
at the lips. Our d is a voiced dental stop. Our k is
a voiceless palatal stop – formed against the hard palate.
The Hebrew Qoph is a voiceless velar stop — formed a—
gainst the velum or soft palate. Now Hebrew has a further series of stops which are formed in the larynx itself and which are termed laryngeals or gutturals. These
sounds may be voiced or voiceless, stops or fricatives.
They are particularly hard for us to reproduce, simply
because we are not used to using our larynx for articu-
lation. An effort should be made however, to distinguish
these sounds as much as possible.

The Remaining Consonants

Print	Writing	Translit.	Name	Pronunciation
א	א	'	Aleph	A glottal stop. The closing of the larynx like ea in "we eat"
ח	חח	ḥ	Ḥeth	A voiceless laryngeal fricative like h but more constricted.
י	ר	y	Yodh	Like y . Silent after vowels.
ע	ע	'	Ayin	A voiced laryngeal fricative like ח but with vocal chords buzzing.
צ	צ	ṣ	Sadhe	An emphatic s.
ץ ש	ץ ש	ś		Form used at end of words.
			Sin	Like s – exactly like Samech (ס)

For convenience of reference the entire alphabet
is here given with transliterations and alternate forms:

t	š	ś	r	q	ṣ	p	'	s	n	m	l	k	y	ṭ	ḥ	z	w	h	d	g	b	'
ת	ש	ש	ר	ק	צ	פ	ע	ס	נ	מ	ל	כ	י	ט	ח	ז	ו	ה	ד	ג	ב	א
ת					פ							כ							ד	ג	ב	
			ץ	ף				ן	ם		ך											

Peculiarities of the Stops – Beghadh-Kephath Letters

As already noted, there are six letters in the
alphabet which are pronounced either as stops (hard) or
as fricatives (soft) according to their position. In
English there is a difference in meaning between "bat"
and "vat" but in Hebrew the b sound and the v sound (ב
and ב) make one letter or phoneme. בן and בן are the
same word. The six Hebrew letters which have a variant
fricative pronunciation are: Beth (ב), Gimel (ג), Daleth
(ד), Caph (כ), Pe (פ), and Tau (ת). For convenience in
remembering them, they have been formed into the word
Beghadh-Kephath (בגד־כפת), and are called the Beghadh-
Kephath letters. To indicate that one of these letters

is hard, a dot is inserted in the middle called a Dagesh lene or hardening dot. This particular kind of dot is never used in any letter except these six and these letters always have it when they are not preceded by a full or half vowel. Either a full vowel or a half vowel – to be studied soon – will soften a following Beghadh-Kephath letter.

Doubling of the Consonants – Dagesh Forte

In Hebrew, the consonants when doubled are not written twice as they are in English. Rather the letter is written once and a dot called Dagesh Forte (strong or doubling dot) is inserted in the middle of the letter concerned to indicate the doubling. This doubling dot is to be sharply distinguished from the hardening dot already learned. The doubling dot may be used with practically all of the letters (it can even be used with the six stops or Beghadh-Kephath letters) and simply means that the letter is to be read twice. The pronunciation should reflect the double letter. When the six stops are doubled, they are also hardened in pronunciation.

As to the use of the Dagesh Forte or doubling dot, it is used if possible when the spelling requires it. But it is important to remember that it can not be used unless the letter to be doubled is preceded by a full vowel and followed by at least a half vowel.

Contrast this rule with the rule above that a Dagesh Lene may be used only in the six stops and is demanded when they are preceded by no vowel at all. To distinguish a Dagesh Forte from a Dagesh Lene, look before the dotted letter. If you find a full vowel there, the Dagesh is Forte; if you do not, it is Lene.

The Definite Article

Hebrew, like Greek has no indefinite article, and a noun is assumed to be indefinite unless made definite in some way as by prefixing the definite article. This definite article, similar to our word "the", consists of the single letter He (ה) prefixed to the beginning of the word. It regularly takes a pathah under it and regularly causes the first letter of the word to be doubled. If this letter is one of the four laryngeals, (א, ה, ח, and ע), or the letter Resh (ר), it cannot be pronounced double and therefore, as we shall see, special rules will apply. Some other cases occur where the accent conditions require a slight modification, but normally the article will be written thus: הַ‎ּ . For instance, if סוּס is "a horse," הַסּוּס is "the horse." מֶלֶךְ is "a king" so הַמֶּלֶךְ

is "the king." "A son" is בֵּן (with Dagesh Lene), so "the son" is הַבֵּן (with Dagesh Forte).

The Sign of the Object

An ordinary verbal sentence - one using a finite verb - is written with verb first, subject next, and object last. This object when definite is usually marked by the particle אֵת or ־אֶת . A noun is definite if it has the article, or if it is a name, or if it is in a genitive relation yet to be studied. An indefinite object is not marked by אֵת . Of course the אֵת is not translated.

The Half Vowel or Shewa

A short indistinct vowel sound something like our 'ᵒ' in "Democrat" is marked by the two dots ְ under a letter called vocal shewa. The same two dots are used under a letter which ends a syllable and then they indicate no sound at all. In this case, they are called silent shewa. The two kinds of shewa can be distinguished by rules to be studied later. We may note here that an initial shewa is always vocal. A vocal shewa is transliterated by a small e above the line; the silent shewa is not transliterated.

Vocabulary (The names for practice, not memorization)

אָדָם	'ādām	Adam	אָב	'āḇ	father (Abijah -Jah is a father)
אַבְרָם	'aḇrām	Abram	מֶלֶךְ	mɛlɛḵ	king (Elimelech-God is a king)
תֶּרַח	tɛraḥ	Terah	כֹּהֵן	kōhen	priest (cf. the common Jewish name)
שִׁמְעוֹן	šim'ōwn	Simeon	סֵפֶר	sep̄ɛr	book (Kirjath Sepher - city of a book)
יְהוּדָה	yᵉhūwḏāh	Judah	בַּת	baṯ	daughter (Bathsheba - daughter of sheba
יוֹרָם	yōwrām	Joram	מָקוֹם	māqōwm	place
שָׂרָה	śārāh	Sarah	כָּתַב	kāṯaḇ	he wrote
צִיּוֹן	ṣiyyōwn	Zion	שָׁפַט	šāp̄aṭ	he judged (Jehosha- phat-Jehovah judged
יְהוֹשָׁפָט	yᵉhōwšāp̄āṭ Jehoshaphat		יְהֹוָה	LORD	Artificial Masoretic writing pronounced 'ᵃḏōnāy

Exercises

A. Translate and practice reading aloud:

הַמֶּלֶךְ אָב 1.   שָׁפַט יְהֹוָה אֶת־הַבַּת 2.   כָּתַב הַמֶּלֶךְ אֶת־הַסֵּפֶר 3.

hassep̄ɛr 'ɛt hammɛlɛḵ kāṯaḇ habbaṯ 'ɛt 'ᵃḏōnāy šāp̄aṭ 'āḇ hammɛlɛḵ

‏4. שָׁמַר שִׁמְעוֹן אֶת־הַסּוּס: 5. הַבֵּן אָב: 6. אָדָם אָב:

’ab ’ādām   ’ab habben   hassūws ’et šim‘ōwn šāmar

‏7. פָּקַד יְהוָה אֶת־שָׂרָה: 8. זָכַר הַמֶּלֶךְ אֶת־יְהוֹשָׁפָט: 9. כָּתַב

kātab yᵉhōwšāpāt ’et hammɛlɛk zākar   śārāh ’et yhwh pāqad

‏אֶת הַסֵּפֶר: 10. שָׂרָה בַּת:

bat śārāh hasseper ’et

B. Transliterate, translate and practice reading:

‏1. פָּקַד יְהוָה אֶת־צִיּוֹן: 2. שָׁפַט הַכֹּהֵן אֶת־הַמָּקוֹם: 3. הַמֶּלֶךְ

‏בֵּן: 4. זָכַר יְהוּדָה אֶת־הַבַּת: 5. שָׁמַר אֶת־יְהוֹשָׁפָט: 6. זָכַר

‏שִׁמְעוֹן אֶת־הַכֹּהֵן: 7. זָכַר הַמֶּלֶךְ אֶת־צִיּוֹן: 8. צִיּוֹן מָקוֹם:

‏9. פָּקַד דָּוִד אֶת־נָד: 10. שָׁמַר הַכֹּהֵן אֶת־הַסּוּס: 11. כָּתַב

‏שֵׁם אֶת־הַסֵּפֶר: 12. זָכַר מֹשֶׁה בַּת: 13. זָכַר יוֹרָם אֶת־הַבֵּן:

‏14. שָׁמַר יְהוָה אֶת־צִיּוֹן: 15. פָּקַד יְהוָה אֶת־תֶּרַח: 16. דָּוִד

‏הַמֶּלֶךְ: 17. נָד בֵּן: 18. כָּתַב סֵפֶר: 19. שָׁפַט מָקוֹם:

C. Translate into Hebrew:
1. Judah is a father. 2. Abram is the king. 3. Simeon visited the daughter. 4. Moses wrote a book. 5. Terah guarded a son. 6. The LORD visited Zion. 7. Jehoshaphat is a king. 8. The Priest remembered Zion. 9. A father guarded the horse. 10. A king remembered the daughter.

Lesson 2 – The Perfect of the Regular Verb

The Hebrew has only two tenses, which are usually called the Perfect and the Imperfect. The Participle also does duty as a kind of tense sometimes. The tenses are not entirely parallel to our English tenses which regard the time of an action – whether past, present, or future – as the important thing. The Hebrew tenses seem rather to consider the completion of the action as important – whether complete, in process of being done, or still to be completed. However, in the majority of cases we may translate the Perfect by our English Past-I killed, the Imperfect by our Future – I shall kill, and the Participle in this usage by our Present – I am killing.

The different persons of the pf. are not indicated by separate personal pronouns as in English. Rather they are indicated by inflection as in Greek or Latin. In the pf. certain letters and vowel points are added to the end of the verbal stem. These endings are really vestigial remains of the personal pronouns and are called sufformatives. They are of two kinds – one beginning with a consonant, the other beginning with a vowel, called consonantal and vocalic sufformatives respectively. The consonantal sufformatives of the pf. sing. for the verb קָטַל meaning "to kill" are:

קָטַלְתִּי I (masc. or fem.) have killed   (sufformative תִּי-)

קָטַלְתָּ thou (masc.) hast killed . . .(sufformative תָּ-)

קָטַלְתְּ thou (fem.) hast killed . . .(sufformative תְּ-)

The third fem. sing. has a vocalic sufformative which we shall learn later, and the third m. s. has no sufformative, being קָטַל "he killed."

Further Remarks on the Alphabet

It is well at the first to form habits of accuracy in reading and writing the Hebrew letters. Note the following letters which are easily confused:

בּ and כּ Beth and Caph. The base line of the Beth extends at the lower right.

ד and ר Daleth and Resh. Daleth is made with two strokes. It has an extension at the upper right.

ה and ח He and Heth. The top line of Heth extends over at both ends. He is open at the upper left.

פ and ת Pe and Tau. Pe has the base line. Final Pe (ף) extends well below the line.

ס and ם Samech and Final Mem. The lower corners of the final Mem are square. Ordinary Mem (מ)is clear.

Vocabulary

מָלַךְ	mālak to reign (root of מֶלֶךְ)	בַּיִת	bayit house (Bethel – house of God)
שָׁבַר	šābar break in pieces	דָּבָר	dābār word
סָפַר	sāpar count (related to סֵפֶר)	שָׁנָה	šānāh year (fem.) (Rosh Hashanah –head of the year)
לָכַד	lākad take, capture	מִשְׁפָּט	mišpāt judgment (root: שָׁפַט)
שָׁכַן	šākan dwell	בְּהֵמָה	behemāh cattle (f.)(cf.Job 40:15,Behemoth,beast)

Exercises

A. Write the four forms of the pf. which we have learned for each of the above five verbs, translating in each case.
B. Write the article with each of the above five, nouns, translating in each case.

C. Translate and practice reading in Hebrew:

קָטַלְתִּי 1. :אֶת־הַסּוּס: 2. מָלַךְ הַכֹּהֵן: 3. שָׁבַרְתָּ אֶת־הַבַּיִת:

habbayit 'ɛṭ šāḇartᵉ hakkōhen mālak̲ hassūws'ɛṭ qāṭaltiy

4. לָכַד מֶלֶךְ אֶת־הַמָּקוֹם: 5. שָׁפַטְתָּ מִשְׁפָּט: 6. סָפַרְתִּי: 7. קָטַל

qāṭal sāpartiy mišpāṭ šāpattā hammāqōwm 'ɛṭ mɛlɛk lāḵad̲

8. שָׁכַן דָּן: 9. כָּתַבְתָּ דָּבָר: 10. שָׁכַן תֶּרַח: גָּד אֶת־הַבְּהֵמָה:

tɛraḥ šāḵan dāḇār kāṭaḇtᵉ dān šāḵan habbᵉhemāh 'ɛṭ gād̲

D. Translate and practice reading in Hebrew:

1. מָלַךְ מֶלֶךְ: 2. זָכַר הַמֶּלֶךְ אֶת־הַדָּבָר: 3. שָׁמַרְתָּ אֶת־הַבְּהֵמָה:

4. פָּקַד דָּוִד: 5. שָׁבַרְתָּ אֶת־הַבַּיִת: 6. מָלַךְ הַמֶּלֶךְ: 7. לָכַדְתִּי

8. הַמֶּלֶךְ אָב: 9. קָטַל בַּת: 10. כָּתַבְתָּ סֵפֶר: אֶת־הַבַּיִת:

11. שָׁבַר יְהֹוָה אֶת־צִיּוֹן: 12. סָפַרְתִּי בְּהֵמָה: 13. שָׁכַנְתִּי:

14. מָלַךְ הַבֵּן: 15. כָּתַבְתָּ אֶת־הַדָּבָר: 16. לָכַד הַכֹּהֵן אֶת

הַבְּהֵמָה: 17. פָּקַדְתְּ בַּת: 18. זָכַרְתָּ אֶת־צִיּוֹן: 19. שָׁמַר

שִׁמְעוֹן: 20. זָכַר הַמֶּלֶךְ אֶת־הַדָּבָר:

E. Translate into Hebrew:
1. I dwelt. 2 Thou (f.) hast written a book. 3. The son
reigned. 4. The LORD has broken the house. 5. Thou (m.)
hast captured the place. 6. I have killed a father. 7. Thou
(f.) hast visited a son. 8. Thou (m.) hast remembered the
word. 9. The king guarded cattle. 10. The LORD visited Zion.

The Perfect of the Regular Verb (cont.)

As has been said, the different endings of the
pf. indicate the different persons. It can readily be
seen that if these endings are consonantal, they will
merely have the effect of adding another syllable, and the
vowels of the stem will remain practically unchanged. The
forms given above show no changes in the stem vowels except that the silent shewa is written just before the
ending. The 1st common plural is similar. However, in
the 2nd pl. masc. and fem. the syllables added are of so
great weight that the first vowel of the form is slurred
and drops to a vocal shewa. Somewhat the same phenomenon
can be seen in English. The word "demon" has a distinct e, but we habitually slur it when the ending is
added in "demoniac." We should say in Hebrew terminology
that the e has dropped to a shewa. These heavy or "grave"
sufformatives frequently change the first part of the

word to which they are attached causing the first vowel to drop to a shewa. The other consonantal sufformatives are:

קְטַלְנוּ we (m. or f.) have killed . . .sufformative נוּ ‎ ‐

קְטַלְתֶּם ye (m.) have killed . . . . . sufformative תֶּם ‐

קְטַלְתֶּן ye (f.) have killed . . . . . sufformative תֶּן ‐

There are only two vocalic sufformatives in the perfect. Since they are only vowels added to the stem, they are attached directly, not making an extra syllable. They do, however, cause the vowel just before the ending to be slurred so that the final added vowel can be pronounced more easily. In general, a vocalic sufformative causes the vowel of the second radical to become a vocal shewa:

קָטְלָה she has killed . . . . sufformative הָ ‐

קָטְלוּ they (m. or f.) have killed . sufformative וּ ‐

All the above sufformatives should be learned thoroughly and skill acquired in attaching them to any verb. The paradigm of the pf. tense is as follows:

(תִּי) קָטַלְתִּי I killed   (נוּ) קָטַלְנוּ we (m.or f.) killed

(תָּ) קָטַלְתָּ you (m.s.) killed (תֶּם) קְטַלְתֶּם you (m. pl.) killed

(תְּ) קָטַלְתְּ you (f.s.) killed (תֶּן) קְטַלְתֶּן you (f.pl.) killed

(–) קָטַל he killed   (וּ) קָטְלוּ they (m.or f.)killed

(הָ) קָטְלָה she killed

In the use of these forms we should remember to put the verb first in a verbal sentence and to make the verb agree with the subject in number and gender.

Vocabulary

קָבַר	bury	לֶחֶם	bread, food (Bethlehem - house of bread)
לָמַד	learn (Talmud - book of Jewish learning)	זָהָב	gold
רָדַף	pursue	כֶּסֶף	silver, money
כָּשַׁל	stumble	אָדָם	mankind, man (Adam - man)
שֵׁם	name	דֶּרֶךְ	way, road

Exercises

A. Write the complete perfect of the above verbs.

B. Translate and practice reading aloud:

1. ‏קְבַרְתֶּם אֶת־הַכֹּהֵן: 2. ‏רָדְפָה שָׂרָה אֶת־הַמֶּלֶךְ: 3. ‏רְדַפְנוּ

4. ‏לָמַדְתְּ אֶת־הַדָּבָר: 5. ‏כָּשַׁלְתֶּן: 6. ‏כָּתְבוּ סֵפֶר: אֶת־יְהוֹשָׁפָט:

7. רָדַפְנוּ אֶת־הַבַּת: 8. שָׁמְרָה הַבַּת אֶת־הַסּוּס: 9. פָּקְדוּ מָקוֹם:

10. קָבְרוּ אֶת־הַכֹּהֵן: 11. לְמַדְתֶּם דָּבָר: 12. כָּתַבְנוּ אֶת־הַסֵּפֶר:

13. שָׁמַר יְהוָה אֶת־צִיּוֹן: 14. קָבְרָה הַבַּת אָב: 15. זָכְרוּ

אֶת־יְהוָה: 16. לָכַדְתָּ אֶת־הַזָּהָב: 17. בָּשַׁל הַכֹּהֵן: 18. שִׁמְעוֹן

אָב: 19. קְטַלְנוּ בְּהֵמָה: 20. מְלַכְתֶּם: 21. שָׁבְרוּ בַּיִת:

22. שָׁפְטָה הַבַּת מִשְׁפָּט: 23. סָפַרְתִּי אֶת־הַבְּהֵמָה: 24. זָכְרָה

בַּת אָב: 25. שָׁמַרְתְּ אֶת־הַמֶּלֶךְ: 26. רָדְפָה שָׂרָה אֶת־הַבַּת:

C. Translate into Hebrew:

1. Ye (f.) have remembered the word. 2. We have buried
the son. 3. They have pursued the cattle. 4. Ye (m)
have written a word. 5. The king stumbled. 6. Ye (f)
have learned the book. 7. The daughter visited the
place. 8. They have learned the word. 9. She h a s
buried the priest. 10. They have pursued a man.

Lesson 3 – The Hebrew Noun

We have learned several nouns, most of which
have been masculine singular, but Hebrew like many languages marks by special inflection the singular and plural,
masculine and feminine. These marks consist of appropriate
endings which, in turn, usually change the pointing of
the body of the word. It is easy to learn the distinctive
endings, but the vowel changes within the word are often
intricate. Fortunately it is possible to recognize the form
of a noun by its ending in most cases and so the changes
in the pointing of the word become important in Hebrew
composition which is not our main purpose just now.

The masc. noun has no ending in the sing. In
the pl. its ending is ִים . as in cherubim for cherubs,
seraphim for seraphs, etc. The fem. sing. ending (when
the gender is marked) is ָה as in many fem. names like
Deborah, Hannah, etc. The fem. pl. is וֹת as in Lord
of Sabaoth – Lord of hosts. These endings applied to
"horse" and "statute" (a fem. noun) are as follows:

horse	horses	statute	statutes
סוּס	סוּסִים	חֻקָּה	חֻקּוֹת

Of course, not all nouns are as regular as these examples.
Many fem. nouns – especially when the meaning of the noun
is fem. as אֵם "mother" – are masc. in form. These nouns,
however, are usually fem. in form in the pl. There is
no neuter gender. The masc. sometimes serves. For ab-

stract ideas, names of organs of the body, names of cit-
ies and countries, etc. the fem. is usually chosen. Some
masc. nouns have fem. endings in the plural. These irregularities can easily be recognized if the above endings are kept clearly in mind.

The Construct State (to indicate a genitive relation)
　　　　Hebrew, having no genitive case, uses a special
form of the noun, called the construct state, to indicate
ownership. Instead of altering the possessing noun as in
Greek, the noun before it, the thing possessed, is shortened and made dependent on the possessor. This shortened
form of the possessed noun is called the construct state.
It may be thought to include our English preposition "of."
Thus, "son of a king" is expressed by "son-of" (the construct state of "son"), and "a king." The noun possessed
(called the ruling noun) is regarded as dependent upon
the possessing noun (ruled noun, our gen.) after it and
therefore there can be no intervening conjunction, preposition or other word except the article.
　　　　Rules for forming the construct state are involved and can not be taken up here. In general the construct state is, if possible, shorter than the normal
or "absolute state." In many masc. sing. nouns the abs.
and const. states are alike. But the m.pl.abs., if it be
regular, always has a regular m.pl.const. and the regular
f.sing.abs. likewise always has a corresponding regular
f.sing.const. The f.pl.abs. and const. endings are alike. The endings are as follows:

	m.s.	m.pl.	f.s.	f.pl.
const. ending	none	׳..	ﬨ_	וﬨ
const. state	horse of סוּס	horses of סוּסֵי	statute of חֻקַּת	statutes of חֻקּוֹת

Because the possessed noun in the const. state
is so completely dependent on the possessor noun following, it shares the definiteness or indefiniteness of the
latter. *A noun in the construct state before a definite
noun is also definite* per se, without using the article.
The construct state, therefore, never takes the article.
Thus, "the statute of the king" is: חֻקַּת הַמֶּלֶךְ and "a
statute of a king" is: חֻקַּת מֶלֶךְ and "the son of the
father of the house" is: בֶּן אַב הַבַּיִת . Hebrew has no
direct way of saying, "a son of the king." The s. construct
states for some common nouns are as follows:

abs.	בְּהֵמָה	שָׁנָה	כֹּהֵן	זָהָב	בֵּן	אַב	מִשְׁפָּט	מָקוֹם	דָּבָר	בַּיִת
cons.	בֶּהֱמַת	שְׁנַת	כֹּהֵן	זְהַב	בֶּן (1)	אַב	מִשְׁפַּט	מְקוֹם	דְּבַר	בֵּית

(1) For a more common form cf. p. 35.

Vocabulary

כָּרַת cut, cut off   בְּרִית covenant (f)-used with כָּרַת in idiom 'make a covenant''

שָׂרַף burn (cf. seraph)   עֶבֶד servant (Ebed-melech-servant of the king)

עָבַד serve (cf. עֶבֶד)   אִישׁ man (Ish-baal-man of Baal) (const. like abs.)

דָּם blood (Aceldama- field of blood)   אִשָּׁה woman, wife (const. אֵשֶׁת)

אָח brother (Ahijah- a brother is Jah) (const. אֲחִי)   אֱלֹהִים God (used with sing. vb. to refer to the true God) (const. אֱלֹהֵי)

Exercises

A. Write the pf. of the first two verbs above.

B. In the phrase "the horse of the king" substitute for "horse" each of the nouns we have learned thus far.

C. Translate and practice reading aloud:

1. שָׁפְטוּ הַמְּלָכִים אֶת־אֲחִי הַכֹּהֵן: 2. קָטְלָה אִשָּׁה בֶן־אִישׁ:

3. לָמַד עֶבֶד אֱלֹהִים אֶת־הַדָּבָר: 4. כָּרַת כֹּהֵן יְהוָה בְּרִית:

5. סָפַרְתְּ אֶת־שְׁנוֹת הַמְּלָכִים: 6. שָׂרְפוּ הַכֹּהֲנִים אֶת־מְקוֹמוֹת

צִיּוֹן: 7. עֲבַדְנוּ אֶת־מַלְכֵי בֵית דָּוִד: 8. כָּרַתִּי בְּרִית:

9. פָּקַד אִישׁ אֶת אַב הַמָּקוֹם: 10. לָמְדוּ הַכֹּהֲנִים אֶת־חֻקּוֹת

הַמְּלָכִים: 11. עֲבַדְתָּ אֶת־בְּנֵי אָדָם: 12. סָפְרוּ מַלְכֵי בֵית

דָּוִד אֶת־זְהַב הַבַּיִת: 13. רָדְפָה אֵשֶׁת עֶבֶד הַמֶּלֶךְ אֶת־אַב הַבַּת:

14. שָׂרַפְתְּ אֶת־לֶחֶם אִישׁ הַמָּקוֹם: 15. סְפַרְתֶּם אֶת־כֶּסֶף הַבַּיִת:

16. זְכַרְתֶּם אֶת־שְׁנַת יְהוָה: 17. כָּתְבוּ כֹּהֲנֵי הַמָּקוֹם אֶת

חֻקַּת יְהוָה: 18. קָטַל אַב אִישׁ אֶת־סוּסֵי עַבְדֵי יְהוָה:

19. כָּשַׁל אָדָם: 20. שָׁפַטְנוּ אֶת־דָּם עֶבֶד הַמֶּלֶךְ:

D. Translate into Hebrew (not using vowel points in the body of pl. nouns or in const. forms if doubtful):

1. We have served the priests of Zion. 2. A father of a man has burnt the house. 3. Ye (m) have cut a covenant. 4. The kings of the place have judged the blood of the father of the daughter. 5. The wife of the son has cut off the house of the road. 6. The servant of the king has learned the word of the LORD. 7. Thou (f) hast written the statutes of the books. 8. The kings have remembered the father of the woman of the house. 9. The daughter killed the cattle of the kings. 10. I burned the kings.

Lesson 4 - Prepositions, Laryngeals, etc.

Inseparable Prepositions and the Conjunction

Three letters, having the force of prepositions are attached to the beginning of nouns. The letter Waw (ו) is attached in the same way and means "and" or but." All these four letters are attached simply by putting a vocal shewa under them. These inseparable prepositions are: בְּ "in" or "with" (in the instrumental sense); כְּ "as" or "like"; לְ "to" or "for." 'Like a father" is: כְּאָב , "To a son" is: לְבֵן , "In a place" is: בְּמָקוֹם , "A king and a priest" is: מֶלֶךְ וְכֹהֵן . We shall learn later how to combine these inseparable prepositions with the article in a phrase like "to the horse." It should be noted that there are other prepositions which stand alone and do not share the peculiarities mentioned above. מִן "from" is used thus: מִן הַסּוּס 'from the horse."

The conjunction "and" or "but" (ו), being a vowel letter has one peculiarity not shared by the three inseparable prepositions. Before a labial (ב, מ, פ, or another ו), or before a word with shewa under the first consonant, the pointing of the conjunction changes from ו to וּ . Thus: "and a house" וּבַיִת , "and a king" וּמֶלֶךְ, "and the word of the king" וּדְבַר הַמֶּלֶךְ .

Peculiarities of the Laryngeals (Gutturals)

As has been noted (p.6), the laryngeals א,ה,ח, and ע as well as the letter Resh (ר) can not be doubled. There is a phonetic reason for this peculiarity - they could not easily be pronounced double, just as the x of English can not double because we can not easily pronounce it so. Instead of doubling, the laryngeals tend to lengthen the preceding vowel so as to keep the syllable value about what it ought to be. Thus if a laryngeal should be doubled, it lengthens the preceding short vowel to a corresponding long vowel. This phenomenon is called "compensatory heightening." For example, if we wish to place the article before אָדָם , we can not use the He with a pathah under it and the next letter doubled, because the Aleph can not double. Instead, the pathah before the laryngeal will lengthen to qames.(1) 'The man" is הָאָדָם . Regularly the pathah changes to qames, the hiriq, to sere, and the qibbus to holem. Compensatory heightening of the vowel is especially important, because it is necessary in reading to apply the principle in the reverse. A laryngeal will be seen with a long vowel before it, but the form can only be deciphered if it is viewed as a short vowel with Dagesh Forte.

(1) Sometimes before ה,ח, or ע the article is הֶ, Ges.p.111

A further complication arises in the case of some of the laryngeals where even compensatory heightening is not done. In these cases no Dagesh appears nor is the preceding vowel lengthened. The doubling is regarded as being implied and the phenomenon is called implicit doubling or virtual strengthening. It occurs most often with Heth, frequently with He, and occasionally with Ayin.

A second peculiarity of laryngeals is that they never take a vocal shewa under them – and only seldom a silent shewa. The vocal shewa, being an indistinct vowel sound, is rejected for a more distinct sound to go with the laryngeal which is apparently difficult enough already. These in-between sounds are called compound shewas, or hateph vowels and are three in number: hateph pathah (_ָ) hateph seghol (ֱ), and hateph qames (ֳ). The hateph pathah is the most common and should be used in the exercises when one is in doubt as to which one is correct. These hateph vowels are, for our purposes, all pronounced just like the vocal shewa and count as a half vowel in rules which we have learned. They are usually transliterated by the a, ɛ, and o written above the line, thus: אֱלֹהִים ʼɛlōhiym .

A third peculiarity of the laryngeals is less predictable yet. The strong laryngeals (ה, ח, and ע) prefer a pathah or at least a A class vowel before them. They often alter a previous vowel to pathah and sometimes change even a following vowel to the pathah. We shall not learn which vowels may thus be changed, but only notice that it frequently occurs. Further if such a laryngeal is at the end of a word, and if the vowel preceding it is an unchangeable vowel not of the A class, an extra vowel, pathah, is slipped in ahead of the laryngeal in pronunciation. This pathah furtive, as it is called, is put under the final laryngeal, but pronounced before it, thus: רוּחַ rūwaḥ .

The Vowel Letters

Four of the Hebrew letters, א, ה, ו, and י, are called vowel letters. As noted already in the alphabet, their peculiarity is that they are pronounced when they have a vowel after them, but are silent when no vowel follows. They therefore never have a silent shewa under them and are not pronounced at the end of a word. Thus, we write קָטַל but the same form in a verb with final Aleph is בָּרָא . We say the Aleph has "quiesced" into the preceding vowel and lengthened it. Quiescing regularly causes this lengthening. The He usually acts as a vowel letter. Final consonantal ה is marked by a dot called Mappiq: הּ

Vocabulary

דָּרַשׁ seek, require of (Midrash-Jewish study)

בָּרָא create (note quiescent א in בָּרָאתָ etc.)

שָׁבַת cease, rest (cf. Sabbath)

שַׂר prince (cf. Israel)

יוֹם day (pl. יָמִים today: הַיּוֹם. cf. Yom Kippur)

חֶרֶב (f) sword, pl. חֲרָבוֹת

אֶרֶץ (f) earth, land (pl. אֲרָצוֹת with art. הָאָרֶץ)

רוּחַ (f) breath, wind, spirit

שָׁמַיִם heavens, sky (a pl. form const. is שְׁמֵי

לֹא not. Used in verbal sentences before word negated.

Exercises

A. Write בָּרָא in the pf. remembering where quiescence occurs. Write שָׁבַת in the pf. remembering to double the ת in forms like שַׁבְתִּי .

B. Put the preposition "in" and the conjunction וֹ "and" (also meaning "but") on each of the above nouns.

C. Translate and practice reading aloud:

1. דָּרְשָׁה הָאִשָּׁה אֶת דְּבַר אֱלֹהִים בְּבֵית: 2. קָטְלוּ אֶת־מַלְכֵי הָאָרֶץ וְאֶת־הָעֲבָדִים בְּחֶרֶב וְלֹא שָׁבָתוּ: 3. בָּרָא אֱלֹהִים אֶת־הַשָּׁמַיִם וְאֵת הָאָרֶץ: 4. דְּרַשְׁתֶּם אֶת־אֱלֹהֵי הַשָּׁמַיִם וְלֹא זְכַרְתֶּם אֶת־שֵׁם יְהוָה: 5. שָׁבַר אֱלֹהִים אֶת־מְקוֹמוֹת הָאָרֶץ וְלֹא שָׁבְתָה בְּרִית יְהוָה: 6. הַיּוֹם עֲבַדְתֶּם כְּעֶבֶד וּקְטַלְתֶּם אֶת־הָאָח בְּחֶרֶב: 7. בָּרָאתָ אֶת־הָאָרֶץ וְאִישׁ: 8. מָלַכְתָּ בִּשָּׁמַיִם: 9. כָּתַבְתְּ לְכֹהֵן וְלֹא בָּשַׁל: 10. דְּרַשְׁנוּ אֶת־שֵׁם יְהוָה וּדְבַר מֶלֶךְ: 11. שָׁפַט אֱלֹהֵי הַשָּׁמַיִם אֶת הַמָּקוֹם בְּמִשְׁפָּט וּבְצִיּוֹן מָלַךְ: 12. שָׁכַנוּ הָאָח וּמֶלֶךְ בְּבֵית הַכֹּהֲנִים: 13. לֹא לָבַדְתְּ אֶת־סוּסֵי הָאִשָּׁה וְאֶת־בְּהֵמַת הָעֲבָדִים: 14. כָּתְבָה רוּחַ יְהוָה אֶת־דְּבַר אֱלֹהִים בְּסֵפֶר: 15. בָּרָאתָ אֶת הַשָּׁמַיִם בְּרוּחַ יְהוָה: 16. פָּגַר הָאֱלֹהִים אֶת־הַיָּמִים וּשְׁנוֹת אָדָם: 17. בָּשְׁלוּ בְּהֵמַת הַכֹּהֲנִים בְּדֶרֶךְ הַמֶּלֶךְ: 18. לָמַדְנוּ אֶת־שֵׁם הָאִישׁ בְּסֵפֶר: 19. לֹא כָּרַתָּ אֶת־הַבְּרִית: 20. פָּקַדְתָּ אֶת־בֵּית יְהוָה:

D. Translate into Hebrew:

1. We have sought God. 2. The LORD has created earth and heaven. 3. She killed the priest in the name of the LORD. 4. We have buried the king in the land of the priest of the LORD. 5. The gold is like silver and the word of the king is like wind. 6. We rested today according to (כְּ) the statute of the LORD. 7. We dwelt in Zion.

Lesson 5 Derived Parts of the Verb

The Hebrew verb is conjugated not only in the simple form that we have studied, but also in derived forms called "stems." Some of these stems are roughly equivalent to passive voices in other languages. But some of the stems are used differently from any phenomenon in English. They are, in fact, used to alter somewhat the meaning of the verb. The basic stem which we have studied is called "Qal" from קַל meaning "simple." The six other stems are named from their base forms. One stem intensifies the meaning of the Qal; another is a causative; another is reflexive. The Qal, the intensive, and causative each has a passive. The paradigm verb formerly was פָּעַל "to make" but this verb was not really suitable because it is irregular in some respects. We now use קָטַל "to kill." But the stems were named long ago after the 3 ms. pf. of the verb פָּעַל and the names still are used. The names do serve to indicate the vowels of the basic form of each stem and should be learned carefully. The seven stems with their base forms and meanings are:

Qal	Piel	Pual	Hiphil	Hophal	Niphal	Hithpael
קָטַל	קִטֵּל	קֻטַּל	הִקְטִיל	הָקְטַל	נִקְטַל	הִתְקַטֵּל
plain	intensive	passive of Piel	causative	passive of Hiph.	passive of Qal	reflexive of Qal
kill	slaughter	be slaughtered	cause to kill	be caused to kill	be killed	kill oneself

Two rules for the formation of certain stems are so useful and so universal in application that they should be learned thoroughly. They even apply to the other tenses and forms still to be memorized: (1) *In the Piel, Pual, and Hithpael, the middle or second radical is always doubled* (except, of course, when it is a laryngeal in which case the rules for heightening the preceding vowel apply), (2) *The Hiphil, Hophal, and the perfect and participle of the Niphal always have a silent shewa under the first radical.* Remember not to count the preformative letters in applying these rules, but only the three consonants of the verbal root. It should also be noted that the vowel under the preformative ה of the Hophal is a Qames-Hatuph or short "o." This explains why the "o" is used in the name "Hophal."

It now remains for us to learn the perfect tense in all of these stems. To do so we merely take the basic form given above and attach the consonantal and vocalic

sufformatives that we have already learned for the Qal.
Two simple rules will show how each form is to be made:
(1) *Addition of consonantal sufformatives causes the vo-*
wel under the second radical to be Pathah. (2) *Addition*
of vocalic sufformatives causes the vowel under the se-
cond radical to drop to a vocal shewa, except in the Hiphil
where the long Hiriq does not change. The paradigm is:

	Qal	Piel	Pual	Hiphil	Hophal	Niphal	Hithpael
Base Form	קָטַל	קִטֵּל	קֻטַּל	הִקְטִיל	הָקְטַל	נִקְטַל	הִתְקַטֵּל
1 cs.	קָטַלְתִּי	קִטַּלְתִּי	קֻטַּלְתִּי	הִקְטַלְתִּי	הָקְטַלְתִּי	נִקְטַלְתִּי	הִתְקַטַּלְתִּי
2 ms.	קָטַלְתָּ	קִטַּלְתָּ	קֻטַּלְתָּ	הִקְטַלְתָּ	הָקְטַלְתָּ	נִקְטַלְתָּ	הִתְקַטַּלְתָּ
2 fs.	קָטַלְתְּ	קִטַּלְתְּ	קֻטַּלְתְּ	הִקְטַלְתְּ	הָקְטַלְתְּ	נִקְטַלְתְּ	הִתְקַטַּלְתְּ
3 ms.	קָטַל	קִטֵּל	קֻטַּל	הִקְטִיל	הָקְטַל	נִקְטַל	הִתְקַטֵּל
3 fs.	קָטְלָה	קִטְּלָה	קֻטְּלָה	הִקְטִילָה	הָקְטְלָה	נִקְטְלָה	הִתְקַטְּלָה
1 cp.	קָטַלְנוּ	קִטַּלְנוּ	קֻטַּלְנוּ	הִקְטַלְנוּ	הָקְטַלְנוּ	נִקְטַלְנוּ	הִתְקַטַּלְנוּ
2 mp.	קְטַלְתֶּם	קִטַּלְתֶּם	קֻטַּלְתֶּם	הִקְטַלְתֶּם	הָקְטַלְתֶּם	נִקְטַלְתֶּם	הִתְקַטַּלְתֶּם
2 fp.	קְטַלְתֶּן	קִטַּלְתֶּן	קֻטַּלְתֶּן	הִקְטַלְתֶּן	הָקְטַלְתֶּן	נִקְטַלְתֶּן	הִתְקַטַּלְתֶּן
3 cp.	קָטְלוּ	קִטְּלוּ	קֻטְּלוּ	הִקְטִילוּ	הָקְטְלוּ	נִקְטְלוּ	הִתְקַטְּלוּ

Do not learn this paradigm. Rather, learn the basic forms,
the endings, and the method of addition of sufformatives.
Stress translation of forms rather than mere memorization.

        It should be carefully noted that the vowel
pointings in the above forms are not equally important.
Special characteristics of some letters and special accent situations will cause minor irregularities in the
treatment of certain vowels. The main characteristics
of each form, however, will be unchanged. Thus the 3 ms.
perfect Piel is given as קִטֵּל but occasionally it is
קִטַּל. The doubled middle radical still indicates that the
form is a Piel. In general the first vowel is characteristic; so also are the doubling of the middle radical in
the Piel, Pual, and Hithpael and the silent shewa under
the first radical of the Hiphil, the Hophal, and the pf.
and part. Niphal (cf. the first two rules on p.18). Note
also that if a stem has no preformative, it must be either Qal, Piel, or Pual. The הִת of the Hithpael is quite
distinctive. We may remark that the preformative הִ can
hardly ever be confused with the article הַ because the
latter is followed by the mark of doubling, the former by

a silent shewa. The student should train himself to look
for these main marks and should not be confused by lesser
departures from the normal forms.

The translations of the derived stems given on
p.18 are to be regarded as only approximate and sometimes
the sense of the derived stems may only be learned by
study of the individual cases. Sometimes, indeed, the
Piel does not especially intensify the meaning, but is
only used as a means of deriving a verb from a very common noun. Thus דִּבֶּר "speak" is a derivative from דָּבָר
"a word" and is only used in the Piel and Pual. We call
these verbs "denominative" and they are most frequently
made by using the Piel and Pual, though the Hiphil and
Hophal are also sometimes used. Frequently the Hiphil
can not easily be recognized as a causative because the
causative idea is thought of as inherent in the verb.
Such a verb will only be used in the Hiphil and Hophal.
For example, נָגַד probably means "be conspicuous," basically, but it is only used in the Hiphil and Hophal in
the meaning "declare." Seldom is one verb used in the
seven stems and if it is, the meaning in some of the derived stems is probably unusual. A good example is בָּרַךְ
which means "kneel" in the Qal, "bless" in the Piel, and
"cause to kneel" in the Hiphil. The Hithpael in this
case is reflexive of the Piel, and means either "bless
oneself" or "be blessed." Of course the meanings of the
passive stems bear a regular relation to the meanings of
the active stems and hereafter if it is said that a verb
has a certain meaning in the Piel or Hiphil, it will be
understood that the Pual or Hophal will have the corresponding passive meanings if they are possible.

Vocabulary

דָּבַר	speak (in Piel)	עַיִן	(f) fountain,eye (cons. עֵין cf.Endor-fountain of Dor)
כָּפַר	make atonement (P.cf.Yom Kippur-day of atonement)	עַם	people (const. עַם cf. Ammi-my people, Hos.2:1)
בָּקַשׁ	seek,search (P.)	קוֹל	voice, sound
בָּרַךְ	kneel (Q),bless (P) (cf. Berachah-blessing)	נֶפֶשׁ	soul, person,life (f. the pl. is נְפָשׁוֹת)

Exercises

A. Write the complete pf. of קָטַל and בָּרַךְ (remember to use
compensatory heightening where needed).

B. Practice reading and rapid translation of the following:

1. קָטַלְתָּ 2. הִקְטַלְנוּ 3. נִקְטַל 4. קְטַלְתֶּן 5. קָטַלְתִּי 6. הָקְטְלוּ

7. הִקְטִילָה 8. נִקְטְלוּ 9. הִתְקַטַּלְתִּי 10. קָטַלְנוּ 11. קְטַלְתֶּם

12. קָטְלָה 13. קְטַלְתְּ 14. הָקְטַל 15. קְטֹל 16. קְטַלְנוּ 17. הִקְטַלְתָּ

18. נִקְטַלְתֶּן 19. הִתְקַטְּלוּ 20. הָקְטְלָה 21. הִתְקַטַּלְתֶּם 22. הִקְטִילוּ

23. הִתְקַטַּלְנוּ 24. נִקְטַלְתְּ 25. הִתְקַטֵּל 26. קָטַלְתִּי 27. קֻטְּלוּ

28. הָקְטַלְתְּ 29. נִקְטְלָה 30. קֻטְּלוּ 31. הִקְטַלְנוּ 32. נִקְטַלְתִּי

33. קָטְלוּ 34. קֻטַּל 35. הִקְטִיל 36. קָטַלְתָּ 37. קְטַלְתְּ 38. הָקְטַלְתֶּם

39. נִקְטַלְנוּ 40. קְטֹלָה 41. הָקְטַלְתָּ 42. קֻטַּל 43. קְטַלְתֶּן 44. הִקְטַלְתְּ

45. הִקְטִילוּ 46. קְטַלְתָּ 47. הָקְטַלְתָּ 48. קְטֹלָה 49. נִקְטַלְתֶּם 50. קֻטַּל

C. Practice reading and rapid translation:

1. הִזְכִּירוּ 2. נִפְקְדָה 3. כְּתַבְתֶּם 4. הֻשְׁמַטְנוּ 5. נִשְׁמַרְתָּ 6. הָמְלְכוּ

7. שָׁבַרְתִּי 8. הִסְפִּירָה 9. הֻלְבַּדְתָּ 10. הָשְׁבַּנְתִּי 11. הִתְקַבְּרֻהֶם

12. בֻּקַּשְׁתֶּם 13. דִּבַּרְנוּ 14. הֻלְמַדְנוּ 15. רֻדַּפְתֶּן 16. הֻבְשְׁלוּ

17. בֵּרַכְתִּי 18. הִתְבָּרַתְנוּ 19. עֻבַּדְתֶּם 20. כֻּפְּרָה 21. הֻשְׁרַפְתָּ

22. דִּבֶּר 23. הִבְרִיךְ 24. הִדְרִישׁוּ 25. בֹּרַכְתָּ 26. נִבְרֵאתָ

27. הָשָׁבַּתִּי 28. בֻּקַּשְׁנוּ 29. כֻּפְּרוּ 30. הִתְבָּרַכְנוּ

D. Translate the following sentences:

1. בֻּקַּשְׁנוּ אֶת־הָעַיִן הַיּוֹם: 2. דִּבַּרְתִּי לְעַם הָאָרֶץ בְּקוֹל:

3. כִּפֶּר יְהֹוָה לְנַפְשׁוֹת הָאָדָם: 4. הִבְרִיכָה אֵשֶׁת הַמֶּלֶךְ אֶת־הָאִישׁ

וְאֶת־הָעֶבֶד בְּבָיִת: 5. הִתְבָּרַכְתִּי בְּשֵׁם יְהֹוָה וּבְקוֹל בֵּרַכְתִּי אִשָּׁה:

E. Translate into Hebrew:

1. We have spoken with a voice like the voice of the kings.
2. She caused the cattle to kneel at (ל) the fountain of
the priests of the place. 3. They have made atonement for
(ל) the people of the land by (בּ) the blood of the cattle.
4. Thou (m) hast blessed thyself in the name of the God
of the heavens. 5. Thou (f) hast not rested in the day
of God and not hast thou been blessed.

Lesson 6   Use of the Vocal Shewa, etc.

The Vocal Shewa and Hatephs

Due to difficulty in pronunciation, Hebrew never
has two vocal shewas in a row. The first one changes to
a full vowel, usually Hiriq, but regularly Pathah if it is
adjacent to a laryngeal. In using this rule remember that
a shewa under the initial consonant of a word is always
vocal, and the shewa under the second radical of a form
of a verb ending in a vocalic sufformative is always vocal.
Likewise there is never a vocal shewa and a Hateph vowel

in a row; the first of the pair changes to the full vowel corresponding to the Hateph vowel. Thus הֲבַר and בְּ are בִּדְבַר, עֲבָדִים and בְּ are בַּעֲבָדִים. Not only will the shewa-Hateph vowel combination change according to the above rule, but also in a similar way occasionally a full vowel-Hateph vowel combination will change so that the full vowel matches the Hateph. Thus the Hiphil of עָבַד becomes הֶעֱבִיד where the short Hiriq under the preformative changes to match the Hateph under the first radical, a laryngeal. This latter case is found most often in the Hiphil, Hophal, and the Niphal perfect and Participle, also the Qal imperfect (yet to be learned) of verbs having the first radical a laryngeal. Typical forms are: Hiphil הֶעֱבִיד, Hophal הָעֳבַד, and Niphal נֶעֱבַד.

An additional irregularity occurs when the second of this full vowel-half vowel combination is a vowel letter, י or א. In this case, the weak letter with a weak vowel under it sometimes loses its vowel completely and quiesces into the preceding vowel thus lengthening it. For example, a form (still to be learned), יִקְטֶל with the conjunction וְ becomes not וְיִקְטֶל but וַיִּקְטֶל. Also אֱלֹהִים and בְּ become not merely בֶּאֱלֹהִים but בֵּאלֹהִים. At other times the quiescing does not occur, as in the Hiphil of אָכַל "to eat" which is הֶאֱכִיל. Much of the above is only intended as a help to the reading of the Hebrew for there is too great irregularity for its application to Hebrew composition by a beginner.

Assimilation of the Nun

In many languages certain letters are occasionally assimilated to the following ones and changed in character. The very word "assimilate" comes from the Latin "ad" and "similis." In bringing the words together the d has been assimilated to the following letter doubling it. In Hebrew, the Nun almost always assimilates when it precedes another consonant with no vowel sound between. When the Nun thus precedes another letter with only a silent shewa under the Nun, the Nun is assimilated to the following consonant thus doubling it. A Nun practically never has a silent shewa under it. The only important exception to the above rule is the case of verbs like שָׁכֵן having Nun as the third radical. In these verbs the Nun is kept without change. But, as we shall see later, in verbs like נָגַד with Nun in the first position, the Nun is assimilated wherever it would have silent shewa under it and in consequence the next consonant doubles. Thus also the preposition מִן "from" may be attached to a noun directly, in which case the Nun coming immediately before another consonant will be assimilated and the next consonant doubled. Thus, "from a house" is מִבַּיִת, "from a horse" is מִסּוּס. However if the letter that should be doubled is a laryngeal, it will refuse the dot and take compensatory heightening or implicit doubling. Thus, "from a father" is מֵאָב. The preposition can also stand alone in which case no assimilation occurs, and it always stands alone when the noun has the article, thus: מִן הַבַּיִת.

Use of the Adjective

Adjectives in Hebrew take the same endings of gender and number as the nouns, but they have no construct state.[1] As in English, there are two usages - attributive and predicate. Attributive, or limiting adjectives are those which modify a noun or pronoun, as "good" in "the good man." Predicate adjectives are those which complete the predicate in a nominal sentence, as "good" in "the man is good." The rules for their use in Hebrew are:

(1) Attributive adjectives follow the nouns they modify and agree therewith in number, gender, and definiteness. Thus, "the good man" is הָאִישׁ הַטּוֹב (טוֹב meaning "good"), but "the good woman" is הָאִשָּׁה הַטּוֹבָה, and "the good horses" is הַסּוּסִים הַטּוֹבִים.

(2) Predicate adjectives may either follow or precede the noun they go with and they agree therewith in number and gender, but not necessarily in definiteness, thus:

"the good man" הָאִישׁ הַטּוֹב   "the man is good" טוֹב הָאִישׁ
"a good man" אִישׁ טוֹב   "a man is good" טוֹב אִישׁ

Vocabulary

לָמַד	learn (Q) teach (P)	גָּדוֹל	great (cf. Gedaliah - great is the Lord)
לָחַם	fight (in N only)	מִלְחָמָה	(f) war, battle (from לָחַם)
אָכַל	eat (Q) consume, as by fire or sword(P)	טוֹב	good (cf. Tobiah - good is the Lord, Yah)
עָמַד	stand (pointed in Hi. and Ho. like אָכַל)	מִן	from

Exercises

A. Write לָמַד in the Piel and Pual, לָחַם in the Niphal, אָכַל and עָמַד in the Hiphil and Hophal.

B. Write in Hebrew: a) The good man b) The man is good c) The good woman d) The woman is good e) The good horses f) The horses are good g) The good statutes   h) The statutes are good. (טוֹב does not change its vowel with the addition of endings)

C. Attach מִן to the nouns in the previous vocabulary.

---

(1) Unless used as a noun, e.g. "the good woman of" טוֹבַת

D. Translate and practice reading aloud:

1.לְמַדְתָּ 2.נִלְחַמְנוּ 3.אֲכַלְתֶּם 4. הָעֶמְדוּ 5. כִּפַּרְתִּי 6.הִתְבָּרְכָה

7.הֶאֱכַלְנוּ 8.הֶעֱמַדְתָּ 9. בִּקַּשְׁתִּי 10.נִבְרֵאתֶם 11.וּמִלְחָמָה 12.הָעָם

13.מֵעַיִן 14. וּבְחֶרֶב 15. לַאֲחִי 16. וּמֵרוּחַ 17. לִשְׁמִי 18. וּבָאלֹהֵי

E. Translate and practice reading aloud:

1.נִלְחֲמוּ אֶת־הַמִּלְחָמוֹת הַגְּדוֹלוֹת בִּמְלָכִים טוֹבִים: 2. לְמַדְתֶּם מִכֹּהֲנֵי

הָאָרֶץ הַטּוֹבִים וְלֹא אֲכַלְתֶּם בְּחֶרֶב אֱלֹהִים: 3. טוֹבִים הַכֹּהֲנִים

וּדְבַר הַמְּלָכִים גָּדוֹל: 4. נִלְכַּד הַמָּקוֹם הַטּוֹב כִּדְבַר יְהֹוָה:

5. בִּקַּשְׁתֶּם אֶת־הָדָם מֵאֵשֶׁת הָאִישׁ הַטּוֹב: 6. הֶאֱבִיל אֱלֹהֵי הַשָּׁמַיִם

אֶת־הַמֶּלֶךְ הַגָּדוֹל כְּבֶהֱמַת הָאָרֶץ: 7. הִתְבָּרַכְתִּי בֵּאלֹהֵי הַשָּׁמַיִם

וְלֹא שָׁבַתִּי מֵחֻקוֹת הַכֶּפֶר הַטּוֹב: 8. הָאָרֶץ לַיהֹוָה וּשְׁמֵי הַשָּׁמַיִם

לֵאלֹהִים: 9. רָדְפוּ הַמְּלָכִים הַגְּדוֹלִים אֶת־הָאִישׁ מִמִּלְחָמָה גְדוֹלָה

לְמָקוֹם הָעַיִן: 10. הָעֶמְדוּ בְּדַרְכֵי יְהֹוָה הַטּוֹבִים:

F. Write in Hebrew:

1. We have taught the good priests from the books of the
LORD.   2.They have fought in the great battle of the LORD
with words (דְּבָרִים) and not with swords (חֲרָבוֹת).   3. I
spoke the word to the brother of the good woman. 4. Ye(m)
have eaten from the bread of the land, but not have you
taught from the book. 5. The place was captured from the
kings of the place in the year of the great battle.

Lesson 7   The Imperfect of the Regular Verb

As explained above (p.8), the remaining tense
of the Hebrew verb, the imperfect, is usually translated
by our future. It consists of a different set of attached letters, called afformative, some of which precede and
others of which follow the basic form. These afformatives must be thoroughly learned so as to recognize the
various persons quickly and accurately no matter what the
verb may be. They are attached to the basic forms according to rules to be studied later. They are:

1 cs	---אָ	I shall		1 cp	---נָ	We shall
2 ms	---תָּ	You(ms) will		2 mp	תָ----וּ	You (mp) will
2 fs	תָ----ִי	You(fs) will		2 fp	תָ----נָה	You (fp) will
3 ms	---יָ	He will		3 mp	יָ----וּ	They (m) will
3 fs	---תָּ	She will		3 fp	תָ----נָה	They (f) will

Unfortunately, the basic stem forms of the imperfect are not all like those we have learned. Only the
Pual, Hophal, and Hithpael stem forms are like the perfect
throughout the paradigm. The impf. basic forms of all the
stems (really the infinitive construct forms) are:

Qal	Piel	Pual	Hiphil	Hophal	Niphal	Hithpael
קְטֹל	קַטֵּל	קֻטַּל	הַקְטִיל	הָקְטַל	הִקָּטֵל	הִתְקַטֵּל

Note that the doubling of the middle radical continues in
the Piel, Pual, and Hithpael. Also the silent shewa under the first radical of the Hiphil and Hophal is still
found. The shewa under the Tau of the Hithpael is also
silent.

The following characteristics of the different
stems should be mastered as they give the key to all the
forms remaining to be learned (infinitives, imperfects,
imperatives, and participles);

(1) In the Piel, the first radical has a Hiriq in the
perfect and a Pathah in all other forms. Preformatives
are added with a shewa in both Piel and Pual.

(2) In the Pual, Hophal, and Hithpael, the perfect
stem vowels continue throughout all the forms.

(3) In the Hiphil, the preformative has a Hiriq in
the perfect and a Pathah in all the other forms.

(4) In the Niphal there is a Nun preformative in the
perfect and participle. Elsewhere the first radical is
doubled (due to the assimilation of the Nun) and it has
a Qames under it.

The first two rules on p.18 still apply - a) The
Piel, Pual, and Hithpael double the second radical. b) The
Hiphil; Hophal, and the perfect and participle Niphal, and
the impf. Qal have silent shewa under the first radical.
The last four stems are preformative stems and always have
a preformative letter of some kind; the first three do
not except in the impf. and in certain participles.

These rules do not allow us to reproduce the
exact form in every instance. In fact, in most cases they do
not say at all what is under the second radical. But
these rules cover the most important characteristics of
each verb form and even apply, with some modifications,
to the irregular verbs. They should be mastered.

As to the attaching of the sufformatives of the
imperfect, remember the rule for vocalic sufformatives -
they cause the vowel of the second radical to drop to a
shewa, except that the long Hiriq of the Hiphil is retained. There is only one consonantal sufformative(נָה)
and the vowels under its second radical are like those
of the basic form with slight exceptions in the Hiphil

and Niphal. The personal preformatives of the imperfect replace the ה of the basic form in the last four stems. They are merely added to the base form in the first three. When this preformative has a Hiriq, the א of the 1 cs, being a laryngeal, changes the vowel to Seghol; when it has a shewa, the change is to Hateph Pathah. Applying these rules we have the following paradigm:

	Qal	Piel	Pual	Hiphil	Hophal	Niphal	Hithpael
1 cs	אֶקְטֹל	אֲקַטֵּל	אֲקֻטַּל	אַקְטִיל	אָקְטַל	אֶקָּטֵל	אֶתְקַטֵּל
2 ms	תִּקְטֹל	תְּקַטֵּל	תְּקֻטַּל	תַּקְטִיל	תָּקְטַל	תִּקָּטֵל	תִּתְקַטֵּל
2 fs	תִּקְטְלִי	תְּקַטְּלִי	תְּקֻטְּלִי	תַּקְטִילִי	תָּקְטְלִי	תִּקָּטְלִי	תִּתְקַטְּלִי
3 ms	יִקְטֹל	יְקַטֵּל	יְקֻטַּל	יַקְטִיל	יָקְטַל	יִקָּטֵל	יִתְקַטֵּל
3 fs	תִּקְטֹל	תְּקַטֵּל	תְּקֻטַּל	תַּקְטִיל	תָּקְטַל	תִּקָּטֵל	תִּתְקַטֵּל
1 cp	נִקְטֹל	נְקַטֵּל	נְקֻטַּל	נַקְטִיל	נָקְטַל	נִקָּטֵל	נִתְקַטֵּל
2 mp	תִּקְטְלוּ	תְּקַטְּלוּ	תְּקֻטְּלוּ	תַּקְטִילוּ	תָּקְטְלוּ	תִּקָּטְלוּ	תִּתְקַטְּלוּ
2 fp	תִּקְטֹלְנָה	תְּקַטֵּלְנָה	תְּקֻטַּלְנָה	תַּקְטֵלְנָה	תָּקְטַלְנָה	תִּקָּטֵלְנָה	תִּתְקַטֵּלְנָה
3 mp	יִקְטְלוּ	יְקַטְּלוּ	יְקֻטְּלוּ	יַקְטִילוּ	יָקְטְלוּ	יִקָּטְלוּ	יִתְקַטְּלוּ
3 fp	תִּקְטֹלְנָה	תְּקַטֵּלְנָה	תְּקֻטַּלְנָה	תַּקְטֵלְנָה	תָּקְטַלְנָה	תִּקָּטֵלְנָה	תִּתְקַטֵּלְנָה

This paradigm, like that of the perfect, should not so much be learned as applied. The student should understand the main points of each stem and person and be able to recognize the forms for any verb.

The Imperative

The imperative mood may be considered along with the imperfect because it is very similar to it — only shorter. In Hebrew, the imperative is only used in the second person and moreover is not used in the truly passive stems, Pual and Hophal. The Niphal is sometimes used with an active meaning in verbs like לָחַם (1) and therefore may have an imperative. The impv. has exactly the same sufformatives as the impf. 2nd person, but does not use any of the imperfect personal preformatives.

---

(1) It seems clear that the Niphal, described above as passive of the Qal, is basically a reflexive of the Qal or is like the Greek middle voice. There was an old passive of the Qal which has largely dropped out of use. The Hithpael is basically reflexive of the Piel, but as the Niphal more replaced the passive Qal, the Hithpael became more a Qal middle. (cf. Ges. pp.137,141, and 149).

The endings of the imperative are:

2 ms --- 2 fs ־ִי 2 mp ־וּ 2 fp ־נָה

These endings are attached to the impf. basic forms just as the impf. endings were attached. The paradigm is:

	Qal	Piel	---	Hiphil	---	Niphal	Hithpael
2 ms	קְטֹל	קַטֵּל		הַקְטֵל		הִקָּטֵל	הִתְקַטֵּל
2 fs	קִטְלִי	קַטְּלִי		הַקְטִילִי		הִקָּטְלִי	הִתְקַטְּלִי
2 mp	קִטְלוּ	קַטְּלוּ		הַקְטִילוּ		הִקָּטְלוּ	הִתְקַטְּלוּ
2 fp	קְטֹלְנָה	קַטֵּלְנָה		הַקְטֵלְנָה		הִקָּטַלְנָה	הִתְקַטֵּלְנָה

The only departures from the imperfect to be noted are the 2 fs and 2 mp Qal where there would have been two vocal shewas in a row. The first has changed to Hiriq. Also the 2 ms Hiphil is somewhat shorter than the corresponding imperfect form being הַקְטֵל not הַקְטִיל.

For the present it will be sufficient to learn that the impv. in Hebrew is used about as it is in English.

Key Forms

To give practice in writing the verb forms and yet avoid the labor of giving the whole paradigm, certain typical or "key" forms are often selected for special drill. If the forms are chosen that have no sufformative, that have a vocalic sufformative, and that have a consonantal sufformative, all the important variations are represented. The key forms of the pf. may be listed as the 3 ms, 3 cp, and 1 cp; for the impf. and impv., as the 2 ms, 2 fs, and 2 fp.

Combinations of the Article and Inseparable Preposition

We can not say "to the house" by just putting the preposition first, the article next, and the noun last. In this construction a telescoping of the shewa under the preposition and the weak letter ה of the article occurs and the result of this elision is the complete loss of the shewa and ה leaving the preposition with the pointing of the article. The combinations "in the," "to the," and "like the" are thus represented by the preposition with a Pathah under it and the initial letter of the noun doubled. Of course, if this letter is a laryngeal, compensatory heightening or implicit doubling will occur. We should remember that this pointing really includes the article and therefore is not used before a construct state. In that situation, the preposition with only a vocal shewa is used, thus: "to a king" לְמֶלֶךְ but "to the king" לַמֶּלֶךְ

Vocabulary

מָשַׁל rule

שָׁלַח send (Q)send away (P) (cf Siloam, sent, impf.יִשְׁלַח due to ח)

וַיֹּאמֶר and he said (special form usually after perfect)

פָּנִים face, faces (Peniel face of God) לִפְנֵי in front of, before

אֹהֶל tent

שָׁלוֹם peace, welfare (cf.Solomon & Arab greeting "salaam")

עוֹלָם age, eon, eternity

Exercises

A. Write the basic forms of the perfect system and of the imperfect system for מָשַׁל, כָּתַב, and בָּרַךְ.

B. Write from memory the complete impf. and impv.of כָּתַב

C. Make yourself a set of flash cards with the afformatives of the various persons of the pf., impf., and impv. Practice their translation thus: ---א, I shall; תָ---, thou(m) hast; ---נ, we shall or Niphal pf. or ptc.; הָ--, she has or feminine noun; ו---, they have or 2 mp impv. etc.

D. Translate and practice pronunciation:

1. אֶמְשֹׁל 2. נְבַקֵּשׁ 3. תִּלָּחֲמִי 4. בָּרְכוּ 5. יָכְשְׁלוּ 6. יִתְבָּרֵךְ

7. הָשָּׁמֵר 8. אֶדְרֹשׁ 9. הֶעֱבִידוּ 10. לָמַדְנָה 11. דַּבֵּר 12.הִמָּשֵׁל

13.זָכֹר 14. יֵרָדְפוּ 15. אֶתְקַטֵּל 16. נְכַפֵּר 17. יָכֹפַּר 18.נִשָּׁמֵר

E. Translate the following list of sentences into Hebrew forms. Practice using other verbs beside "kill."

1. You (mp) have caused to kill. 2. He will slaughter. 3. They have killed themselves. 4. You (mp) have been killed. 5. I shall be killed. 6. Cause to kill, ye women. 7. He will kill. 8. I shall kill myself. 9. They (mp) will cause to kill. 10.Slaughter, thou man. 11.We shall kill. 12. They have been killed. 13. Cause to kill, thou man. 14. Ye (m) will kill. 15. Slaughter, ye men. 16. I shall be killed. 17.They (m) will kill. 18. Thou (f) wilt be slaughtered. 19.Kill, thou man. 20.I have been killed.

F. Translate the following:

1. יִמְשְׁלוּ הַכֹּהֲנִים וְהַמֶּלֶךְ הַטּוֹב בַּבַּיִת: 2. תִּשְׁלַח אֵשֶׁת הָאִישׁ הַטּוֹבָה אֶת־הַבַּת לָאֹהֶל: 3. דִּבֶּר וַיֹּאמֶר קָטַל אֶת־הַבְּהֵמָה הַגְּדוֹלָה: 4. יִמְשֹׁל אֱלֹהִים לְעוֹלָם בַּשָּׁמַיִם: 5. לֹא יִלָּחֵם שַׂר שָׁלוֹם בְּחֶרֶב: 6. עָמַדְתִּי לִפְנֵי אֱלֹהִים וַיֹּאמֶר שְׁלַח אֶת־הַשַּׂר לַבַּיִת: 7. יִמְשֹׁל יהוה מִן הַשָּׁמַיִם וּמִצִּיוֹן: 8. נִלְמַד שָׁלוֹם לָעָם: 9. שַׁלַּח אֶת־הַבַּת: 10. הָשְׁבַּן אֶת־הַשַּׂר לִפְנֵי הַמֶּלֶךְ בַּבַּיִת: 11. וַיֹּאמֶר אֶשְׁלַח אֶת

עִם הָאֱלֹהִים לֵאלֹהִים: 12. וַיֹּאמֶר לַמְּדוּ אֶת־הָעָם כְּחֻקַּת הַמֶּלֶךְ

הַגָּדוֹל: 13. דִּבֶּר אֱלֹהִים לַכֹּהֲנִים וַיֹּאמֶר תְּבֹרַכְנָה נַפְשׁוֹת

הָעָם: 14. יַאֲכִילוּ אֶת־הָעָם אֶת־הַלֶּחֶם וְלֹא יֵאָכֵל בְּיוֹם הַמִּלְחָמָה:

15. עָמְדוּ בַּבַּיִת וְלִמְּדוּ אֶת־הַדָּבָר הַטּוֹב מִסֵּפֶר יְהוָה: 16. יְבַקֵּשׁ

הַשָּׂר הַטּוֹב אֶת־פְּנֵי יְהוָה: 17. שָׁלוֹם לָעָם הַטּוֹבִים וְלֹא יַעַמְדוּ

עַם הָאָרֶץ בַּמִּלְחָמָה: 18. יִשְׁפֹּט אֱלֹהִים אֶת־הָעֶבֶד הַטּוֹב וְלֹא

יִשְׁבֹּת שֵׁם הָאִישׁ הַטּוֹב מִן לִפְנֵי יְהוָה לְעוֹלָם:

Lesson 8   The Remainder of the Regular Verb

The Participle

The two participles of the Qal are not subject
to rule and should be well learned by themselves. Outside of Qal and Niphal, the participles are formed on the
anology of the basic stem forms of the imperfect. They
are similar to the 3 ms impf., but have מ for a preformative instead of י. The active stems each have an
active participle and the passive stems a passive form.
There is a Qames under the 2nd radical of all passive
participles except the Qal.

The Infinitives

Each stem has two infinitives, the absolute and
the construct. These designations do not have any relation to the abs. and const. states of nouns. Rather they
mean that the abs. inf. is used alone or absolutely in
the sentence, whereas the const. inf. is used in construction with prepositions and other words more like our English infinitive "to kill." The basic stem forms of the
impf. given on p.24 are the construct infinitives. The
absolute infinitives are just like the constructs except
that they have Holem after the second radical in all stems
but the Hiphil and Hophal which have Sere. These forms
complete the paradigm of the regular verb:

	Qal	Piel	Pual	Hiphil	Hophal	Niphal	Hithpael
			The Infinitives				
Abs.	קָטוֹל	קַטֵּל	קֻטֹּל	הַקְטֵל	הָקְטֵל	הִקָּטֹל	הִתְקַטֵּל
Const.	קְטֹל	קַטֵּל	קֻטַּל	הַקְטִיל	הָקְטַל	הִקָּטֵל	הִתְקַטֵּל
			The Participles				
Act.	קֹטֵל	מְקַטֵּל		מַקְטִיל			מִתְקַטֵּל
Pass.	קָטוּל		מְקֻטָּל		מָקְטָל	נִקְטָל	

Syntax of the Participle

The Hebrew participle is used somewhat as our participle in English. It shares some characteristics of a verb and some of an adjective. It is very often used substantively - as a noun. As a verb, it can take an object, but it has no tense determination. The active participles with a subject are frequently used like a present tense - time present to the situation described in the context - thus, "He is killing," "Lot was sitting." The passive participle Qal is used like the Greek perfect passive participle, כָּתוּב "it is written" γέγραπται. This participle seems probably to be the only commonly used form remaining from the earlier passive Qal stem, now not much used. The other passive participles - especially Niphal, but also Pual and Hophal - very often correspond to a Latin gerundive or an English adjective ending in -able or -some: נֶאֱכָל a clean thing "to be eaten" or ceremonially "edible"; נִבְרָא a people "to be created"; נִתְעָב (from תָּעַב "be abhorred") "abominable."

All the participles are often used in nominal sentences: אַבְרָם קֹטֵל אֶת־הַסּוּס "Abram is killing the horse." הָאִישׁ קָטוּל "The man is killed." Here the participle acts like a predicate adjective and must agree accordingly. They are also used in clauses which we would express by a relative: הָאִישׁ הַקֹּטֵל אֶת־הַסּוּס "The man who is killing the horse." Here the participle acts somewhat like an attributive adjective and must agree accordingly. A clearer example of attributive usage would be: הַלֶּחֶם הַנֶּאֱכָל "The edible bread." Finally, the participles may be used substantively and can be subject, object, etc. of a sentence in which case they take the gender and number appropriate to their function: אֲבָרֵךְ מְבָרְכִים אֶת־אַבְרָם "I shall bless the ones who bless Abram." The participles may also be in the construct state: רֹדְפֵי הָאִישׁ "the pursuers of the man" i.e. "those who pursue the man."

It may be helpful in recognizing the plurals, feminines, and constructs of the participles to note that the first half of the form down to and including the second radical does not change with endings, thus: מְקַטְּלִים, מִתְקַטְּלוֹת, נִקְטָלִים, קְטֻלָה. The only exception is the passive Qal participle which drops the Qames to a shewa when endings are attached. Note that the participles very frequently have the article before them. No other part of the verb does. They can also have prepositions, but this is rare.

Syntax of the Infinitive

The inf. abs. is used to emphasize the idea of the verb in the abstract. Its most frequent use is just before a finite verb for emphasis, thus: קָטוֹל תִּקְטֹל "killing thou shalt kill," "thou shalt surely kill." The two verbs are usually in the same stem. Again, the inf. abs. may be used just after a finite verb to indicate either emphasis, as above, or long continuance of action. Occasionally the inf. abs. is used as a substitute for a finite verb with the tense, person, etc. shown by the context.

The inf. const. shares the functions of a verb and a noun. As a verb it may take an object. The time of the action is to be learned from the context. As a noun, the inf. const. may be the subject or object of a verb, as "to serve pleases the king," or it may be used after a noun in the construct state. In these cases it is similar to our English gerund (to be sharply distinguished from the Latin gerundive mentioned above.)

One of the most frequent uses of the inf. const. is in a prepositional phrase like the Greek ἐν τῷ εἶναί με. The preposition precedes the inf. const. and the subject of the clause, if there be a subject expressed, follows. Thus we have an inf. of purpose with ל : לִקְטֹל "in order to kill." The prepositions בְּ and כְּ are very commonly used idiomatically to make a temporal clause: "in his going," i.e. "when he went." בִּקְטֹל אַבְרָם "in the killing of Abram," i.e. "when Abram killed." The preposition בְּ, which is much more frequently used, is more often to be translated "when" whereas כְּ usually means "while." In these forms the vocal shewa becomes silent: לִכְתֹּב to write.

Vocabulary

קָרַב draw near(Q) bring near(P) offer(H) (Corban-offering)

אֶבֶן stone (f) (Ebenezer – stone of help)

זָבַח sacrifice (Impf. יִזְבַּח due to laryngeal)

קֹדֶשׁ holiness

אָמַר say (3ms impf. יֹאמַר,1cs אֹמַר due to א)

קָדֹשׁ holy (Kadesh Barnea – holy place of Barnea)

שָׁמַד be destroyed (N)

הַר mountain (Armageddon – perhaps Mt. Megiddo)

יָם sea (pl. יַמִּים)

עַל upon, above, beside, on the ground of, concerning

נָבִיא prophet

Exercises

A. Write from memory all the inf. and part. of בָּרַךְ.

B. Translate and practice reading aloud:

1. וּמשֶׁה אָמַר לָעָם לִזְבֹּחַ בְּהֵמָה(1)לֵאמֹר הַקְרִיבוּ לֵאלֹהִים:

2. בְּדַבֵּר הַנָּבִיא אֶת־דְּבַר יְהוָה הָעָם לְמֻדִים קֹדֶשׁ: 3. משֶׁה עָמַד

עַל הָאֶבֶן: 4. וַיֹּאמֶר יְהוָה הָהָר קָדֹשׁ: 5. שָׁפוֹט אֶשְׁפֹּט

אֶת־הָעָם הַקְּדֹשִׁים הַיּוֹם עַל הָהָר: 6. יִזְבְּחוּ הָעָם בְּהֵמָה נֶאֱבָלָה:

(1) "saying" (often introduces direct discourse).

7. וַיֹּאמֶר אֱלֹהִים לַנָּבִיא קְרַב לָהָר הַקָּדוֹשׁ: 8. קָדוֹשׁ יְהוָה
וְגָדוֹל בַּקֹּדֶשׁ הָאֱלֹהִים: 9. בִּדְבַר יְהוָה הַשָּׁמַיִם נִבְרְאוּ וּבְרוּחַ
אֱלֹהִים הַיָּם נִבְרָא: 10. שָׁלַח הַמֶּלֶךְ אֶת־הַנָּבִיא בִּבְנֵי יִשְׂרָאֵל:
11. קָרְבוּ הַנְּבִיאִים וְעֹמְדִים עַל הָהָר: 12. קָרַב הַכֹּהֵן וַיֹּאמֶר
לָעָם לִזְבֹּחַ לֵאלֹהִים בְּקֹדֶשׁ: 13. הָעָם אֹמְרִים טוֹבִים מִשְׁפָּטֵי
הַנָּבִיא וּמִשְׁפְּטֵי הַכֹּהֲנִים: 14. דִּבֶּר הַנָּבִיא בְּשֵׁם יְהוָה בְּקוֹל
גָּדוֹל: 15. אָכְלוּ הָאֲבָנִים וְהָאָרֶץ: 16. בְּבַקֵּשׁ הָעָם אֶת־אֱלֹהִים
תִּשְׁבֹּת הָאָרֶץ מִמִּלְחָמָה: 17. אֹהֶל אֱלֹהִים לִפְנֵי הָהָר הַקָּדֹשׁ:
18. שָׁלַח הַמֶּלֶךְ אֶת־הַשַּׂר לִמְשֹׁל לְעוֹלָם: 19. שִׁלַּח הַנָּבִיא אֶת
הָעָם וַיֹּאמֶר אַקְרִיב אֶת־הָאָדָם לַיהוָה: 20. בָּרָא אֱלֹהִים אֶת
הַיַּמִּים אֶת־הֶהָרִים אֶת־הָאֲבָנִים וְאֶת־הָאָרֶץ:

C. Translate the following forms and parse each:

1. נֶאֱכַל 6. יִשְׁלְחוּ 2. מְקָרֵב 3. אָמֹר 4. הַקְרִיב 5. מְשַׁלַּח
7. כְּפָנַי 8. הֶעֱמַד 9. כִּפֵּר 10. הִתְבָּרֵךְ 11. לְעַיִן 12. לְלַמֵּד
13. לַיָּם 15. וּמִלְחָמוֹת 14. הַטֹּבִים

D. Translate into Hebrew:

1. He sent the prophet to sacrifice upon the great stone.
2. Draw near to the man and speak saying (לֵאמֹר) "the
mountain is holy." 3. The LORD will send peace to Zion
forever (לְעוֹלָם). 4. Rule thou (m) in the holy land in
peace. 5. When Abram sent away Lot, Abram was standing
before the LORD.

E. The following lists will be helpful for drill on the
irregular as well as the regular verbs. List A is for
drill on the Qal only; List B covers the whole verb.
Do both lists for כָּתַב.

A	B
a) 3 cp perfect Qal	2 ms imperative Hiphil
b) inf. const. Qal	Niphal participle
c) 1 cs imperfect Qal	3 ms imperfect Piel
d) 2 fs imperfect Qal	2 ms perfect Hiphil
e) Act. part. Qal	inf. abs. Hithpael
f) 2 ms imperative Qal	2 fs imperfect Niphal
g) 3 ms imperfect Qal	3 cp perfect Hophal
h) 2 fp imperfect Qal	1 cs imperfect Hiphil
i) Pass. part. Qal	2 mp perfect Niphal
j) 3 fs perfect Qal	Hiphil participle

Lesson 9   The Waw Consecutive

We have already seen how the Waw with a shewa under it is used as a simple conjunction. The Waw is also used in a special sense with the imperfect tense and in this usage called Waw consecutive or Waw conversive with the imperfect. This Waw consec. with the imperfect can easily be distinguished from an ordinary or conjunctive Waw by the fact that the Waw consec. with the imperfect always has the pointing of the article - that is, it has a pathah under it and the next letter doubled, thus: וַיִּקְטֹל . This Waw cons. also means "and," but in addition it practically always gives the imperfect tense a past meaning: וַיִּקְטֹל means "and he killed." Because of the apparent switch of tenses, the form used to be called Waw conversive. Later it was observed that this form usually occurs in a sequence after a perfect or equivalent form. Characteristic Hebrew style would thus be: קָטַל וַיִּקְטֹר . Still the origin of the form was not satisfactorily explained and several have more recently attempted to show that the idiomatic usage is a relic of a former usage of a tense like our imperfect. The old usage would thus be retained only in the close-knit phrase, Waw with the imperfect. For our purposes we may simply observe that the expression is the characteristic tense of Hebrew narration. It is natural therefore that usually there should stand a perfect at the head of the section, but this is not absolutely necessary.[1] We must notice that if the idiom is changed by insertion of another word between the

---

(1) Z.S.Harris in "Development of the Canaanite Dialects" (pp.45ff), argued that there was an old form, yaqtulu, used for past time and another form used for present and future. This, in brief, is the situation in Akkadian. A qatala form arose, however, due to various influences, and became a tense of complete action. The imperfect as we know it then became the tense or, more accurately, the aspect of incomplete action. The Waw cons. with the impf. is thus considered to retain the old past usage of the yaqtulu tense. Some of this argument rests upon evidence from the Ras Shamra literature and is not all admitted at present.

G.R.Driver in a note in Weingreen's 'Practical Grammar for Classical Hebrew," argues that Hebrew is a composite language and the Waw consecutive with the imperfect as well as a somewhat similar Waw with the pf. are connected with the Akkadian while the ordinary tenses resemble the Aramaean system. Driver makes no attempt

Waw and the verb, we may no longer use the imperfect. Thus, "He killed and he did not bury" is קָטַל וְלֹא קָבַר. Also remember that the pointing of the Waw will change with laryngeals, etc. just as does the pointing of the article. Thus, "and I killed" is וָאֶקְטֹל ; "and I slaughtered" is וָאֶטְבַּח . When a Yodh has a shewa under it in this idiom (or at any time),[1] and should be doubled, the Yodh, being a very weak letter, regularly drops the Dagesh Forte, thus: "and he slaughtered," וַיְטַבַּח .

The Waw consec. with the impf. not only has the pointing of the article, but also tends to attract the accent one step toward the beginning of the form making some changes in the pointing in consequence. These changes will be taken up later for irregular verbs. With the regular verb there is no alteration except in the Hiphil impf. forms without sufformatives. There the long Hiriq changes to Sere under the influence of the Waw consec., thus, יַקְטִיל but וַיַּקְטֵל . Note the similarity of this form to the shortened 2 ms imperative Hiphil.

The rules for the use of the Waw consec. with the impf. are easily learned. But the important thing is to be able to recognize at a glance this very common idiom. We must remember, therefore, that when we see a

---

to explain why this curious and unnecessary mixture has persisted in the classical Hebrew.

C. H. Gordon in his "Ugaritic Handbook," departs somewhat from Z. S. Harris' treatment of the verbal system of the Ras Shamra tablets, but he does say (p.96) that the yaqtulu form is the one usually used for narration. He often prefers to translate it as a historical present. It would seem that, although problems remain for solution, yet the Waw consec. with the impf. is really an idiomatic relic of a former narrative tense or aspect and its similarity to the present imperfect is perhaps coincidental. There are not wanting indications that this old narrative form is preserved in a few other places besides these with Waw consec. After some other particles as אָז, "then;" טֶרֶם, "not yet;" בְּטֶרֶם, "before;" etc. and especially in poetry (cf.Ex.15:6,12,14,15) the old narrative yaqtulu may be preserved. More study may clarify the situation. For an older view of the subject, cf. Ges. p.326ff and S. R. Driver, "Treatise on the Use of the tenses in Hebrew."

(1) This loss of Dagesh Forte in letters having vocal shewa under them also frequently occurs in the liquid ל, the nasals מ and נ, the sibilants, and the emphatic ק. cf. Ges. p.74.

Waw with the pointing of the article, it means (1) that
the form is a Waw consec. with the imperfect, (2) that
the letter right after the Waw is a preformative of the
imperfect and not the first radical of the verb, and (3)
that the form is to be translated in general as if it
were a perfect.

There is also a Waw consec. with the perfect
later to be studied and also an ordinary Waw with the
perfect or imperfect called Waw conjunctive, but these
are less common and can easily be distinguished as they
do not have the pointing of the article.

Irregular Nouns

Some nouns have a form in the plural which is
quite dissimilar from the form in the singular and will
be very confusing unless these irregularities are learned. Since many of these irregular nouns are of the most
common occurrence, at least the following should be memorized:

	father	man	woman	house	son	daughter	day
abs. sing.	אָב	אִישׁ	אִשָּׁה	בַּיִת	בֵּן	בַּת	יוֹם
const. sing.	אֲבִי	אִישׁ	אֵשֶׁת	בֵּית	בֶּן	בַּת	יוֹם
abs. pl.	אָבוֹת	אֲנָשִׁים	נָשִׁים	בָּתִּים	בָּנִים	בָּנוֹת	יָמִים
const. pl	אֲבוֹת	אַנְשֵׁי	נְשֵׁי	בָּתֵּי	בְּנֵי	בְּנוֹת	יְמֵי

An Alternative Feminine Ending

As learned above, the absolute fem. sing. ending is usually הָ— . However, this הָ-- is apparently
a development from an older ־ת--- which was the earlier
indication of the feminine and which reappears in the
const. fem. sing. ־ת=-- and the f. pl. ־וֹת--- . In addition
to the abs. fs. ending הָ-- there is occasionally used an
alternative ending retaining the ־ת---. Its form is ־ת=-–
(changing to ־ת==- in the neighborhood of laryngeals). It
is particularly important in the inflection of participles
but almost always the parallel form הָ---is also in use.
Thus, the Qal act.part.fs.abs. is either קֹטְלָה or קֹטֶלֶת .
The form ־ת=-- is the same in the abs. and const. states.
The Qal act.part.fs.const. therefore is either קֹטֶלֶת or
קֹטְלַת . With a laryngeal   שֹׁלַחַת

The Locative He

The locative He is a suffix הָ- put at the end
of nouns referring to places, occasionally, to indicate
"place to which." It is considered by some to be a remnant of a former accusative case used adverbially.

Vocabulary

שָׁלַךְ	throw, cast (Hi)	מִזְבֵּחַ	altar (from זָבַה) m. but pl. מִזְבְּחוֹת
שָׁחַת	go to ruin (Q), destroy(P), ruin(Hi)	זֶבַח	a sacrifice
עָבַר	cross over, through, or by; transgress	לֵב	heart, inner man, mind
שָׁם	there; שָׁמָּה thither	עֵץ	tree, wood
עִם	with	אֶל	unto, into, towards

Exercises

A. Write the Waw consecutive with the complete impf. in the Qal, Piel, and Hiphil of קָטַל and עָבַר (for 1 cs. Hiphil write וָאַקְטִיל as shortening does not occur in this form.)

B. Parse completely (Giving root, stem, form, gender, number and state) the following participles:

1. לִשְׁלֹה 2. נִשְׁחָתִים 3. מַעֲבִירֵי 4. אֹמֶרֶת 5. מְלַמֵּד 6. בָּרוּךְ

7. מְקֻרָבוֹת 8. שְׁלוּחִים 9. נֶאֱכָלֵי 10. מַעֲמִיד

C. Translate the following and practice reading aloud:

1. עָבַר שֵׁת הָהָרָה וַיַּעֲמֹד לִפְנֵי יְהוָֹה: 2. וַיֹּאמֶר אֱלֹהִים קֹדֶשׁ הַמָּקוֹם: 3. וַיִּקְרַב אַבְרָם וַיַּקְרֵב אֶת־הַבֵּן עַל הַמִּזְבֵּחַ לְזֶבַח אֶל יְהוָֹה: 4. וְלֹא קָטַל אַבְרָם אֶת־הַבֵּן: 5. וַיִּשְׁחַת אֶת־הַמִּזְבֵּחַ עִם הָעֵץ וְעִם הָאֲבָנִים: 6. וַיַּעַבְרוּ מִשָּׁם אֶל הָאָרֶץ הַטּוֹבָה: 7. כְּהַשְׁלִיךְ הָאִשָּׁה אֶת־הַבֵּן וַתַּעֲבֹר הָעַיְנָה וְהַבֵּן מְבַקֵּשׁ אֶת־הַלֶּחֶם: 8. לֵב הָאֲנָשִׁים לִמֵּד אֶת־הַטּוֹב וְהַנָּשִׁים מְלַמְּדִים אֶת־הַבָּנוֹת בְּכָתֵי הָעָם: 9. וָאַעֲבִיר אֶת־הַכֹּהֲנָה הַטּוֹבָה מִשָּׁם וָאַקְרֵב הָעַיְנָה: 10. הַקְרִיבוּ אֶל יְהוָֹה עַל הַמִּזְבֵּחַ הַקֹּדֶשׁ וְלֹא תִזְבְּחוּ בָּנִים: 11. לֵב הָאָדָם לִמֵּד לַעֲבֹר חֻקּוֹת הָאֱלֹהִים וְלֹא יְבָרֵךְ יְהוָֹה אֶת־הָאָרֶץ בְּשָׁלוֹם: 12. וַיְדַבֵּר הַנָּבִיא לֵאמֹר בָּרוּךְ עִם אֱלֹהִים לְעוֹלָם: 13. הָאִשָּׁה מָשְׁלָת עַל הָעָם וַתֹּאמֶר שְׁמֹר אֶת הַחֻקּוֹת: 14. הַבָּנוֹת נִלְחָמוֹת בַּנָּשִׁים וְהַבָּנִים נִלְחָמִים בָּאָבוֹת בָּאֹהָלִים: 15. שָׁחַת אֹשֶׁת אֶת־כָּתֵי הָעִבְרִים חָקַק הָאֱלֹהִים וְלֹא יַעֲמֹדוּ: 16. וַיִּשְׁלְחוּ שָׂרֵי הַמָּקוֹם אֶת־בְּנֵי הַמֶּלֶךְ לִמְשֹׁל עַל הָעָם הַטּוֹב: 17. דִּבְּרוּ הַכֹּהֲנִים לָעָם לֵאמֹר הַלֶּחֶם נֶאֱכָל וְהַזְּבָחִים קְרוּבִים:

18. קָרְבִּי וָאַשְׁלִיךְ אֶת־הָאֲבָנִים עַל הַבַּת לִקְטֹל אֶת־הָאִשָּׁה:

19. וַיִּקְרַב אֶשֶׁת הַכֹּהֵן אֶת־הַמִּנְחָה וַתִּקְרָב לָהָר הַקֹּדֶשׁ לִזְבֹּחַ:

20. טוֹב לֵב הָאָבוֹת אֶל אֱלֹהִים זְבָחִים וַיַּקְרִיבוּ עַל הַמִּזְבֵּחַ:

D. Write in Hebrew:
1. When the king destroys the altar, not will he sacrifice the cattle there. 2. Lot is the one transgressing the statutes of the LORD. 3. The women threw the sacrifice from upon (מֵעַל) the altar in order to burn the son. 4. The wife of the prophet transgressed the statute of the LORD saying (לֵאמֹר), "Destroy the houses of the men of the place." 5. Offer unto God cattle with wood. 6. The fathers drew near to the sea and they cast stones upon the prophet there. 7. The king spoke to the priests and they killed cattle and they offered sacrifices and they sacrificed the cattle upon the altar. 8. The heart of the wife of the king is holy. 9. The men of the place crossed over to the fountain and they destroyed the tents of the sons. 10. The women destroyed the altar and they cast the stones into the sea.

Lesson 10   The Lamedh He Verb

Irregular Verbs in General

In Hebrew there are five classes of irregular verbs which are important. In fact a great number of the verbs which occur in the Old Testament are irregular. Yet when we know the regular verb thoroughly, the irregular verbs do not constitute so much of a problem for there are generally enough of the regular elements of the verb left even in an irregular form to locate it easily. We shall therefore study the irregular verbs from the viewpoint of their irregularities. Notice we are not studying five new conjugations, but only five forms of irregularity caused when ordinary letters are replaced by special letters which drop out or are modified in certain positions. These verbs are usually named from the place in which the irregular letter occurs. Since the old paradigm verb was פָּעַל , the first position was the Pe position, the second the Ayin, and the third the Lamedh position. A Lamedh He (ל"ה) verb, therefore, is a verb with a He in the third or Lamedh position, such as בָּנָה, "build." A more modern nomenclature refers to the positions by number, calling נָצַל a First-Nun (נ-I) verb; קוּם a Second-Waw (ו-II); etc.

The Lamedh He (ל"ה) Verb

The ל"ה verb ends in a He. This He, however, was not original with these verbs, which formerly ended either in a Waw or, more commonly, a Yodh. Therefore they are more properly called Third-Waw, Yodh verbs (ו'-III). It is important to note that the final He is really a false ending added only to carry the final vowel and it is easily lost. It regularly drops or modifies before any other ending is added.[1]

The weakness in these verbs is at the end and therefore, as we should expect, the first part of the verb to and including the second radical is perfectly regular in all forms. The irregularities of the latter part can be summarised under three rules which apply to all stems and are very easy of application:

(1) When there is no sufformative and thus the original ' or ו would have stood at the end of the form, a ה takes its place and the ל"ה verb then ends in הָ- in the perfect, הֶ- in the imperfect, and הֵ- in the imperative.

(2) When there is a vocalic sufformative, it is added on directly to the second radical of the verb. The only exception is the 3 fs. perfect (all stems) where a ת is inserted before the הָ--- to make the form בָּנְתָה instead of בָּנָה. It may be noted that but for this exception the 3 ms. perfect and the 3 fs. would be alike.[2]

(3) When there is a consonantal sufformative, the ל"ה verb has inserted between the second radical and the ending a helping vowel which is -יָ- in the perfect (occasionally -ִי- especially in the passive stems), and in the imperfect and imperative is -ֶי- .

The absolute infinitives are perfectly regular using ה for the third radical. All the construct infinitives end in וֹת-- having this added directly after the second radical.

---

(1) In certain forms of the ל"ה verbs in Ras Shamra the final letter appears as a Yodh. In cases like בָּנַיְתִי where the Yodh is a mere vowel letter, the Ras Shamra tablets do not write it. Where it is consonantal as in the 3 ms. imperfect יִבְנֵי (with a short vowel doubtless at the end), the Yodh is sometimes written. cf. Gordon, op. cit. p.78.

(2) But the ת is really not an insertion. It probably is a remnant of the old feminine ת which appears also in the fs. const. of nouns, מַלְכַּת , and other places.

All participles except the passive Qal end in
הָ‑‑‑ .However, this false ending is removed before any
ending demanded by inflection for number or gender is
added. Thus, "a building man" is בֹּנֶה but "a building wo‑
man" is בֹּנָה and "a builder of" is בֹּנֵה. The endings
act just the same in the derived stems. The Qal passive
participle must be learned by itself: בָּנוּי .Actually it
is the only form in the paradigm which is absolutely reg‑
ular, retaining as it does the old consonantal ' .

Forms of the imperfect with Waw consecutive
cause special difficulty. We saw in the previous lesson
that these have tendency to shorten if there is no suf‑
formative. In the ל"ה verb, this means the final הָ‑
drops. The apocopation of the final הָ‑ occurs in all
seven stems in those forms without a sufformative except the
1 cs. which, as we saw, does not usually shorten in the
regular verb. The dropping of the הָ‑ causes other
changes. If the last two consonants are now left in a
cluster with a silent shewa between them, a helping vowel
or "anaptyctic" vowel is inserted. This helping vowel
is regularly seghol, except that in the neighborhood of a
laryngeal it will be pathah. Thus, "he will build" is
יִבְנֶה but "and he built" is not just וַיִּבֶן but וַיִּבֶן. In
the Piel and Pual this helping vowel is not necessary,
but the doubled middle radical is now left at the end of
the word and therefore the Dagesh Forte drops out. Thus,
יְבַנֶּה but וַיְבַן . The Hiphil takes a helping vowel like
that of the Qal, but the vowel under the preformative
changes to match it. Thus, יַבְנֶה and וַיֶּבֶן . The Hophal
and Hithpael have no special problems being formed quite
like the Qal and Piel respectively. The Niphal alone has
no changes other than the apocopation of the הָ‑ .   In
all these forms the apocopation is accompanied with a re‑
traction of the accent to the syllable beginning with the
preformative. Thus וַיִּבֶן .

Mappiq
A dot called Mappiq is occasionally seen in a
final ה. Like the other Dageshes, the Mappiq indicates
a stronger pronunciation. When it occurs we pronounce
the final ה as a consonant, not a vowel letter. Verbs
which end in such a ה do not follow the above rules at
all. They originally ended in a consonantal h not in w
or y and therefore they are to be treated like any other
verb ending in a laryngeal. Thus "he will be high" is
יִגְבַּה . The ה will prefer a pathah and there will be no
apocopation.

For convenience of reference the key forms and other important forms of בָּנָה "build" are here given:

Perfect

	Qal	Piel	Pual	Hiphil	Hophal	Niphal	Hithpael
3 ms	בָּנָה	בִּנָּה	בֻּנָּה	הִבְנָה	הָבְנָה	נִבְנָה	הִתְבַּנָּה
3 fs	בָּנְתָה	בִּנְּתָה	בֻּנְּתָה	הִבְנְתָה	הָבְנְתָה	נִבְנְתָה	הִתְבַּנְּתָה
1 cp	בָּנִינוּ	בִּנִּינוּ	בֻּנִּינוּ	הִבְנִינוּ	הָבְנִינוּ	נִבְנִינוּ	הִתְבַּנִּינוּ
3 mp	בָּנוּ	בִּנּוּ	בֻּנּוּ	הִבְנוּ	הָבְנוּ	נִבְנוּ	הִתְבַּנּוּ

Imperfect

	Qal	Piel	Pual	Hiphil	Hophal	Niphal	Hithpael
2 ms	תִּבְנֶה	תְּבַנֶּה	תְּבֻנֶּה	תַּבְנֶה	תָּבְנֶה	תִּבָּנֶה	תִּתְבַּנֶּה
2 fs	תִּבְנִי	תְּבַנִּי	תְּבֻנִּי	תַּבְנִי	תָּבְנִי	תִּבָּנִי	תִּתְבַּנִּי
2 fp	תִּבְנֶינָה	תְּבַנֶּינָה	תְּבֻנֶּינָה	תַּבְנֶינָה	תָּבְנֶינָה	תִּבָּנֶינָה	תִּתְבַּנֶּינָה
ו cons.	וַיִּבֶן	וַיְבַן	וַיְבֻן	וַיֶּבֶן	וַיָּבֶן	וַיִּבֶּן	וַיִּתְבַּן

Imperative

	Qal	Piel	Pual	Hiphil	Hophal	Niphal	Hithpael
2 ms	בְּנֵה	בַּנֵּה	- -	הַבְנֵה	- -	הִבָּנֵה	הִתְבַּנֵּה
2 fs	בְּנִי	בַּנִּי	- -	הַבְנִי	- -	הִבָּנִי	הִתְבַּנִּי
2 fp	בְּנֶינָה	בַּנֶּינָה	- -	הַבְנֶינָה	- -	הִבָּנֶינָה	הִתְבַּנֶּינָה

Infinitives

	Qal	Piel	Pual	Hiphil	Hophal	Niphal	Hithpael
abs.	בָּנֹה	בַּנֹּה	בֻּנֹּה	הַבְנֵה	הָבְנֵה	הִבָּנֹה	הִתְבַּנֹּה
const.	בְּנוֹת	בַּנּוֹת	בֻּנּוֹת	הַבְנוֹת	הָבְנוֹת	הִבָּנוֹת	הִתְבַּנּוֹת

Participles

	Qal	Piel	Pual	Hiphil	Hophal	Niphal	Hithpael
act.	בֹּנֶה	מְבַנֶּה		מַבְנֶה			מִתְבַּנֶּה
pass.	בָּנוּי		מְבֻנֶּה	מָבְנֶה		נִבְנֶה	

Vocabulary

עָלָה go up(Q), make go up(Hi) (Elyon-Most High; cf עַל)

עָשָׂה do, make (Q)

צִוָּה command (P)

בָּנָה build (Q) (possibly connected with בֵּן)

כָּלָה be complete(Q), bring to an end (P)

עוֹלָה (f) burnt offering

מַעֲשֶׂה deed, work(such nouns use const. הַ)

מִצְוָה commandment (f)

צֹאן (f) sheep, small cattle

רָשָׁע wicked (used substantively, wicked one)

Exercises

A. Write the key forms of the imperfect with ו cons. for בָּנָה

B. Write the impf. Qal(just like Hi.) and impv. Hi. of עָלָה

C. Write the complete Piel of צָוָה .

D. Translate and practice reading aloud:

1. וַיַּעַל אַבְרָם הָהָרָה וַיִּבֶן מִזְבֵּחַ שָׁם וַיְצַו אֶת־הַבֵּן לַעֲלוֹת

עַל הַמִּזְבֵּחַ: 2. וַיְדַבֵּר אֱלֹהִים אֶל אַבְרָם לֵאמֹר הַעֲלֵה צֹאן

עַל הַמִּזְבֵּחַ לְעוֹלָה וַיַּעַשׂ אַבְרָם כִּדְבַר יְהוָה: 3. וַיְדַבֵּר יְהוָה

אֶל אַבְרָם לֵאמֹר בָּרֹךְ אֲבָרֶךְ אֶת־אַבְרָם וַיְצַו אֶת־אַבְרָם לִשְׁמֹר

אֶת־מִצְוֹת אֱלֹהִים: 4. וַיְכֻלּוּ הַשָּׁמַיִם וְהָאָרֶץ וַיָּבָל אֱלֹהִים בַּיּוֹם

הַקֹּדֶשׁ אֶת־הַמַּעֲשֶׂה: 5. וַיַּעַשׂ אֱלֹהִים אֶת־הָאָדָם וַיְצַו אֶת־הָאָדָם

לִבְנוֹת מִזְבְּחוֹת וְלִזְבֹּחַ צֹאן: 6. בַּעֲבֹר הָרְשָׁעִים חָקָה יִשְׁחָטוּ:

7. יְכַלֶּה אֱלֹהִים אֶת־בֵּית הָרְשָׁעִים וּבֵית הַקְּדֹשִׁים יִבָּנֶה לְעֹלָם:

8. לֹא עָשׂוּ הָאֲנָשִׁים מַעֲשֵׂה קֹדֶשׁ וְלֹא יְבֹרַךְ: 9. הָעֲלָה עֹלַת הַבֹּחֶן

הָעֻשָּׂה כִּדְבַר הָאֱלֹהִים: 10. נִבְנֵית וַתְּכֻלִּי כִּמְצֻנַּת הָרְשָׁעִים:

11. תַּעֲשֶׂינָה הַנָּשִׁים הַמַּעֲלוֹת אֶת־הַזְּבָחִים   טוֹב: 12. אָמַר הָאִישׁ

עֹלֹה עָלִיתִי הָהָרָה הַשָּׂרֵף: 13. עָשִׂינוּ אֶת־מַעֲשֵׂה אֱלֹהִים וְלֹא

כָלִינוּ אֶת־הַבֵּית יְהוָה: 14. נִלְחֲמוּ הַבָּנִים בַּחֲרָבוֹת וַתִּבְנֶינָה

בְּנוֹת הַנָּשִׁים אֶת־הַבָּתִּים: 15. וַיֹּאמֶר אֲכַלֶּה אֶת־אַנְשֵׁי הַמָּקוֹם:

E. Translate into Hebrew:

1. The prophets went up and they commanded the people to do the good. 2. The altar was built and the sacrifice was made. 3. Ye (m) have finished the house. 4. I have certainly offered up the burnt offering which was commanded. 5. We commanded the people to build the houses of the women. 6. The men of the place crossed over thither to sacrifice burnt offerings. 7.When the men cast the stones into the sea, the house will be ruined. 8. The women are sending the books to the wicked priests.

Lesson 11   The Stative Verb

There are a number of verbs called "statives," which are somewhat similar to our intransitive verbs expressing a state rather than describing an action. For example, the verb "be heavy" expresses the state of the subject. These verbs are exactly like the regular verbs in the derived stems, but differ at some important points in the Qal. The important differences between the statives

and the regular verbs is in the imperfect and imperative
Qal, where a pathah replaces the holem; and in the inf.
const. Qal which occasionally has a feminine ending. In
addition to these "pathah statives" there doubtless were
originally some "sere statives" using sere instead of the
holem, but examples of these only remain in irregular
verbs. Key forms of קָדֵשׁ "be holy" in the impf. and impv.
are:

	Imperfect	Imperative
2ms	תִּקְבַּשׁ	קְדַשׁ
2fs	תִּקְדְּשִׁי	קִדְשִׁי
2fp	תִּקְבַּשְׁנָה	קְדַשְׁנָה

The infinitive construct is often feminine - in form only.
This form may be illustrated by דָּבְקָה "to cleave to."
It will be seen that these forms of the stative verb are
quite similar to those of verbs ending in a laryngeal
such as תִּשְׁלַח where the pathah arises for a different reason.

There are less important irregularities found
in some stative verbs in the perfect and participle. Some
verbs like כָּבֵד "be heavy" have a sere in the 3 ms pf.
form. Forms with a sufformative, however are regular. A
very few other verbs like קָטֹן "be small" have a holem
in this second syllable. Such verbs retain the holem
throughout the perfect Qal. The active Qal participle
of these verbs is exactly like the perfect - inasmuch as
both are adjectival in force and have practically the
same meaning. Other statives, like קָדֵשׁ ,have ptc. קֹדֵשׁ
A further word should be said. A verb can not
be recognized always as stative by the meaning, because
of our different habits of thought. We use "love" as a
transitive verb requiring an object. Hebrew uses "love"
as a stative verb describing a condition. So the differences in meaning are not to be emphasized, but the
variant verb forms are to be kept in mind and will have
an important application in the study of irregular verbs.

The Interrogative

Instead of using a question mark at the end,
Hebrew uses a He with a hateph pathah under it at the
beginning of an interrogation. Before a vocal shewa,
the hateph pathah will change to a pathah in order to
avoid two vocal shewas in a row. Also before laryngeals,
the hateph pathah normally changes to either a pathah or

seghol. The He interrogative can be distinguished from the article because it practically never doubles the next letter or has its vowel heightened to a qames. Often the interrogative is not expressed, being implied from the context.

The Negatives

We have learned that לֹא is the negative used for ordinary verbal sentences. A second verbal negative is אַל used somewhat like μη in Greek. It expresses a negative wish or mild prohibition, as "Let not the king say so." This is not used for a negative command. "Thou shalt not kill," is לֹא with the imperfect. אַל is used with the jussive which we shall study later, but which is usually identical with the imperfect — it is shorter if possible and therefore quite like those forms of the imperfect used with Waw consecutive. The negative used in nominal sentences is very common. It is properly a substantive אַיִן meaning "nothing." In the absolute state it may stand removed from its noun, but is more frequently used in the construct state, אֵין just before the noun it negates: "nothing of the book is good." אֵין הַסֵּפֶר טוֹב "Abram was not standing," אֵין אַבְרָם עֹמֵד .

Personal Pronouns in the Nominative

For a complete list cf. Ges. p.105. The forms which should be memorized are:

I   אֲנִי or אָנֹכִי   we נַחְנוּ or אֲנַחְנוּ

thou (m) אַתָּה thou (f) אַתְּ ye (m) אַתֶּם   ye (f) אַתֵּן

he הוּא   she הִיא   they (m) הֵמָּה   they (f) הֵנָּה

Vocabulary

דָּבַק (stative) cleave to   רָכַב (st) ride

לָבֵשׁ (st) put on (clothes, armor, etc.)   עָנָה answer (Q),(different verb in P,afflict)

כָּבֵד (st) be heavy,rich(Q), glorify (P)   וַיֵּלֶךְ and he went, (from הָלַךְ "go")

קָדַשׁ (st) be holy (Q), sanctify (P also Hi)   כֹּל or כָּל־ all,every

רָאָה see (irreg. Q impf. forms: וַיֵּרְא , וַיִּרְא)   כִּי conj., that,because, when; sometimes,if

Exercises

A. Write the impf. and impv. Qal and Hi.of קָדַשׁ and עָנָה.

B. Parse the following forms:

1. מְכַבְּדִי 2. נֶעֱנֵיתִי 3. תִּרְכַּב 4. לָבוּשׁ 5. וַיְצַוּוּ 6. בָּלִינוּ

7. הַעֲבִירִי 8. וּמִזְבְּחוֹת 9. בְּבַרְתֶּם 10. תִּתְקַדַּשְׁנָה 11. לַעֲשׂוֹת

12. הַמַּעֲשִׂים 13. הַמַּקְרִיבִים 14. אֶשְׁלַח 15. יֵרָאוּ 16. בְּדָבְקָה

C. Translate and practice reading aloud:

1. אַבְרָהָם כָּבֵד וַיהֹוָה בֵּרַךְ אֶת־אַבְרָהָם בַּכֹּל: 2. וַיֹּאמֶר לָעֶבֶד

גְּדוֹל הַבַּיִת דַּבֵּר לָאַחִים לְאִשָּׁה לְיִצְחָק: 3. וַיִּתְקַדֵּשׁ הָעֶבֶד

וַיֵּלֶךְ וַיַּעֲבֹר לְבֵית אֲחִי אַבְרָהָם: 4. וַיְדַבֵּר אֶת־כָּל־הַדְּבָרִים

הַדִּבּוּרִים בְּאָזְנָיו: 5. וַיַּעַן אֲחִי אַבְרָהָם וַיֹּאמֶר רָאִיתִי כִּי

עָשָׂה יְהֹוָה גְּדוֹלוֹת וְאֵין קָדוֹשׁ כַּיהֹוָה: 6. וַתִּלְבַּשׁ הָאִשָּׁה

וַתִּרְכַּב עִם הָעֶבֶד לְאֹהֶל אַבְרָהָם: 7. וַתִּדְבַּק בְּיִצְחָק לְעוֹלָם:

8. נִלְחַם דָּוִד וַתִּדְבַּק נֶפֶשׁ בְּנֶפֶשׁ יוֹנָתָן דָּוִד כִּי רָאָה כִּי

הִמְשִׁיל אֱלֹהִים אֶת־דָּוִד: 9. וַיֹּאמֶר אַתָּה טוֹב וַיַּעַן דָּוִד כִּי

יְהֹוָה קָדֹשׁ: 10. וַיַּלְבֵּשׁ יוֹנָתָן אֶת־דָּוִד וַיְכַבֵּד אֶת־דָּוִד:

11. וַיֹּאמֶר הוּא בֶן הַמֶּלֶךְ וַאֲנִי בֶן־דָּוִד כִּי דָּבַק בְּדָוִד:

12. הוּא קָדַשׁ וְהִיא כָּבְדָה: 13. וַיְצַו אֱלֹהִים אֶת הָאֲנָשִׁים

לְדָבְקָה בַּנָּשִׁים לְעוֹלָם: 14. רָאִינוּ אֶת־הַנָּבִיא וַיִּרְכַּב עַל

הַסּוּס: 15. וַיִּירָא הָאִישׁ אֶת־הַנָּבִיא וַיֹּאמֶר כַּבֵּד אֶת־יְהֹוָה:

D. Translate into Hebrew:
1. They (m) were rich, and she is great.   2. The woman
cleaved to the daughters and they rode upon horses to the
fountain. 3. She caused the priest to go up to the house
and he was clothed (Q) with holiness. 4. Sanctify your-
selves (Hith) in the heart and glorify God in deeds.   5. We
are seeing all the works of men and the men are not holy.
6. All of the daughters answered and they said, we destroyed the tents. 7. The woman built the houses and she
saw the tent that it was destroyed. 8. The LORD is riding
upon the heavens and the name of God is honorable (כָּבֵד)
in the earth. 9. And God afflicted the fathers because
they transgressed the commandments. 10. We were caused
to go up to the house of the prophet. 11. The priests
will be clothed with holiness and will do the work of the
LORD. 12. And God appeared (was seen) in the tent and
he spoke to the people by voice.

Lesson 12 The Pe Nun Verb

The Active or Regular Group, Class I

Verbs with Nun in the Pe position (also called First-Nun, ‎נ-I) are irregular in those places where a silent shewa would appear under the Nun. In these places, the Nun assimilates doubling the following letter which is the second radical. As we have learned, there is a silent shewa under the first radical in the Hiphil; Hophal; pf. and part. Niphal; and impf. Qal. In these places of the Pe-Nun verb the Nun will therefore be assimilated doubling the second radical. The verb will be entirely regular throughout the Piel, Pual, and Hithpael and in parts of the Qal and Niphal. The fact that this assimilation occurs frequently must teach us to be on the watch for an unexplained Dagesh Forte in a verb form. It might indicate an assimilated Nun which we must mentally restore before we can locate the form.

The only other peculiarity of these verbs is in the Hophal where, throughout the stem, the Qames Hatuph after the preformative changes to a Qibbus. A skeleton paradigm for ‎נָפַל "fall" is as follows:

	Qal	Piel	Pual	Hiphil	Hophal	Niphal	Hithpael
3 ms pf.	נָפַל	נִפֵּל	נֻפַּל	הִפִּיל	הֻפַּל	נִפַּל	הִתְנַפֵּל
3 ms impf.	יִפֹּל	יְנַפֵּל	יְנֻפַּל	יַפִּיל	יֻפַּל	יִנָּפֵל	יִתְנַפֵּל
2 ms impv.	נְפֹל	נַפֵּל	—	הַפֵּל	—	הִנָּפֵל	הִתְנַפֵּל
Inf. const.	נְפֹל	נַפֵּל	נֻפַּל	הַפִּיל	הֻפַּל	הִנָּפֵל	הִתְנַפֵּל
part. act.	נֹפֵל	מְנַפֵּל		מַפִּיל			מִתְנַפֵּל
pass.	נָפוּל		מְנֻפָּל		מֻפָּל	נִפָּל	

The Pathah Stative, Class II

There are other ‎נ"פ verbs in addition to those above, which bear about the same relation to Class I as stative verbs bear to regular verbs. Class II is just like Class I outside of the Qal stem. In the Qal stem the Pathah statives, typified by ‎נָגַשׁ "approach," are very similar to such ordinary statives as ‎קָדַשׁ "be holy." They also are perfectly regular in the Qal perfect, infinitive absolute, and participles. Irregularities appear in the Qal only in the imperfect, imperative, and infinitive construct. In the imperfect, the Nun is assimilated and in addition there is a Pathah under the second radical: ‎יִגַּשׁ (cf. ‎יִקְדַּשׁ). The imperative also has the characteristic

Pathah under the second radical, but in addition loses the weak Nun entirely: גַּשׁ (cf. קְרַשׁ). The infinitive construct has a feminine form, but having lost the weak Nun it uses the alternative feminine ending and is called a segholate infinitive: גֶּשֶׁת (cf. דִּבְקָה). The paradigm below should be thoroughly learned as these verbs constitute a very important class. Another verb, לָקַח "take" acts exactly as if it were לָקַן , a פ"נ verb of this class and should be noted at this time.

The Sere Stative, Class III

Class III has only one representative, but it is the very important verb, נָתַן "give." It also is regular outside of Qal and in the Qal perfect, infinitive absolute, and participles as well. Indeed it behaves as we should expect, assimilating the third radical Nun before other consonants, e.g. 2 ms Qal נָתַתָּ , Piel נִתַּתָּ , Hiphil הִתַּתָּ ,etc. It will be remembered that other verbs with Nun in the third position do not assimilate it in this way, e.g. 2 ms Qal שָׁכַנְתָּ ,etc.

The irregularities of נָתַן in the Qal imperfect, imperative, and infinitive construct are as follows: The imperfect assimilates the first Nun and has a Sere under the second radical: יִתֵּן (יִנְתֵּן). The impv. also has the characteristic Sere under the second radical, but like Class II drops the weak first Nun: תֵּן . The infinitive construct has a feminine form, but the third radical Nun causes a change from the segholate form expected after analogy to Class II and the result is תֵּת . Actually the third radical Nun has assimilated into the last Tau, but this Tau instead of doubling has made the preceding vowel long making תֵּת instead of תֶּנֶת .

Key forms of irregular parts of the Qal for all the classes are as follows:

	Imperfect			Imperative		
	Class I	Class II	Class III	Class I	Class II	Class III
2 ms	תִּפֹּל	תִּגַּשׁ	תִּתֵּן	נְפֹל	גַּשׁ	תֵּן
2 fs	תִּפְּלִי	תִּגְּשִׁי	תִּתְּנִי	נִפְלִי	גְּשִׁי	תְּנִי
2 fp	תִּפֹּלְנָה	תִּגַּשְׁנָה	תִּתֵּנָּה	נְפֹלְנָה	גַּשְׁנָה	תֵּנָּה

Inf.const. Class I: נְפֹל Class II: גֶּשֶׁת Class III: תֵּת

Use of the Lexicon and Concordance

The vocabularies in connection with the lessons are so arranged that all the verbs and nearly all the nouns used more than 100 times in the Hebrew Bible will

be memorized. It is convenient, however, to use other
less common words in some of the exercises and hereafter
some such words will be used. Valuable practice will be
received in looking these up in a lexicon. Most lexicons
list all nouns under the roots from which they are derived. Parsing the forms and determining the derivation
of nouns is therefore important. Proper names of less
frequent occurrence will be marked in the next few lessons by an asterisk.

The only lexicons suitable at present (1949)
for a serious student are the edition of Gesenius by Brown,
Driver, and Briggs; and the later editions of the same
in German by F. Buhl. Unfortunately all of these are out
of print and scarce.[1] Various other popular lexicons
or older editions of Gesenius can be secured. Brown,
Driver, and Briggs (BDB) may be used as a Hebrew concordance for most of the less common words. Those words for
which it gives all occurrences are marked with a dagger
to show that further reference to a concordance is not
necessary. The other words which are of too common occurrence to be so treated have a subscript number giving
the total number of times they are used. Words so common as these seldom need to be traced through a concordance as the meaning is rather well assured. The standard
concordances are the Englishman's Hebrew and Mandelkern's
Hebrew Concordance. Both of these are expensive, but
well worth having.

Vocabulary

נָפַל   fall (Cl I)   לָקַח   take (Cl II פ"נ ;
                                                 inf. const. קַחַת)

נָגַד   declare (H)   נָתַן   give, put, set (Cl III,
                                                 cf. Nathaniel)

נָצַל   snatch, deliver (H)   נָגַשׁ   approach (Cl II)

נָשָׂא   lift up (Cl II; impf. יִשָּׂא   שָׁמַע   hear (cf. Shemiah)
         inf. const. שְׂאֵת)

מָה   or מַה־ or · מֶה what? (used   אֵם   (f) mother
         in direct or indirect questions)

Exercises

A. Write the complete Qal stem of נָגַשׁ and נָתַן .
B. Write the following list, first for נָגַשׁ then for נָתַן :
1. 1 cs pf. Qal   4. Inf. cons. Qal   7. 2 fs impf. Qal
2. 2 fs impv. Qal   5. 3 fs pf. Piel   8. 3 ms impf. Hiph.
3. 1 cp pf. Niphal   6. 1 cs impf. Qal   9. part. Hophal

---

(1) See preface for later information.

C. Translate with the help of a lexicon:

1. וַיֵּלֶךְ אִישׁ מִבֵּית *לֵוִי וַיִּקַּח אֶת־בַּת *לֵוִי: 2. וַתַּהַר הָאִשָּׁה

וַיִּתֵּן אֱלֹהִים לָאִשָּׁה בֵּן: 3. וַתֵּרֶא אֶת־הַבֵּן כִּי טוֹב וַתִּצְפֹּן

אֶת־הַיֶּלֶד: 4. וַתִּשְׁמַע אֶת־הַבֵּן כִּי בָכָה וַתִּשָּׂא אֶת־הַבֵּן: 5. וַתִּקַּח

תֵּבָה וַתִּתֵּן אֶת־הַתֵּבָה עִם מֹשֶׁה בַּמַּיִם: 6. וַתִּגַּשׁ *מִרְיָם לִרְאוֹת

מָה יֵעָשֶׂה לַיֶּלֶד: 7. וַתֵּלֶךְ בַּת *פַּרְעֹה עִם הַנָּשִׁים לַמַּיִם

לִרְחֹץ וַתֵּרֶא אֶת־הַתֵּבָה וַתֹּאמֶר מָה בַּתֵּבָה: 8. וַתִּשְׁלַח אִשָּׁה

לְהַצִּיל אֶת־הַתֵּבָה: 9. וַתַּצֵּל אֶת־הַתֵּבָה וַתִּשָּׂא אֶת־הַיֶּלֶד וְהוּא

בֹּכֶה: 10. וַתִּגַּשׁ *מִרְיָם וַתֹּאמֶר הַאֵלֵךְ לָקַחַת אִשָּׁה לִשְׁמֹר עַל

הַיֶּלֶד: 11. וַתַּגֵּד אֶל־אֵם הַבֵּן כִּי בַת *פַּרְעֹה נָשְׂאָה אֶת־הַתֵּבָה:

12. וַתִּשְׁמַע אֵם מֹשֶׁה וַתַּגֵּד לָאָב וַיִּפְּלוּ וַיְכַבְּדוּ אֶת־אֱלֹהִים:

13. וַתִּתֵּן בַּת *פַּרְעֹה אֶת־הַיֶּלֶד לָאִשָּׁה וַתֹּאמֶר אֶתֵּן זָהָב

וָכֶסֶף: 14. וַתֹּאמֶר הָאֵם הַאֶקַּח זָהָב וָכֶסֶף לִשְׁמֹר עַל־הַיֶּלֶד:

15. וַתִּפֹּל אֵם מֹשֶׁה לִפְנֵי יְהוָה:

D. Translate into Hebrew:
1. The brother built the house and he approached to the
men and he declared that the house is fallen.   2. And
they said,"Lift up the stones of the house and set a stone
upon a stone." 3. And he took the stones and it was done.
4. And the man fell from upon the horse and the daughter
approached to lift up the man, and she rescued the man
who had fallen. 5. And she said to the mother,"What are
you hearing?"

Lesson 13   The Pe Waw Verb
The third important class of irregular verbs
has the weak and irregular letter at the beginning just
as does the Pe Nun verb. The verbs are more accurately
called First Waw or Yodh verbs (י"ו-I) because most of
them originally had a Waw, but some of them a Yodh in
the Pe position. We shall study the true Pe Waw verbs
first. The two kinds look alike in the lexicons as the
original Waw has been replaced by Yodh in nearly all forms.
Thus יָלַד "bear a child," is truly Pe Waw whereas יָנַק
"suck," is really Pe Yodh.
The true Pe Waw verbs, like the פ"ן verbs have
different classes in the Qal stem, but are all alike in

the derived stems. Irregularities appear when the original Waw of the root coalesces with the vowel of the preformative as follows:

(1) In the Hophal, the Waw combined with the Qames hatuph of the preformative to form a Shureq throughout: הוּשַׁב , הוּשְׁבוּ , יוּשַׁב , מוּשָׁב .

(2) In the Hiphil, the combination[1] resulted in a holem which appears throughout: הוֹשִׁיב , יוֹשִׁיב , מוֹשִׁיב .

(3) In the Niphal pf. and part., the same Holem appears as in the Hiphil and for the same reason: נוֹשַׁב , נוֹשָׁב . But in the rest of the Niphal the original Waw reappears and is doubled as usual with a Qames under it: הִוָּשֵׁב , יִוָּשֵׁב .

(4) The Piel, Pual, and Hithpael are perfectly regular as they are in the Pe Nun verb. They use Yodh as the first radical.

Study the skeleton paradigm for the derived stems:

	Piel	Pual	Hiphil	Hophal	Niphal	Hithpael
3 ms pf.	יִשֵּׁב	יֻשַּׁב	הוֹשִׁיב	הוּשַׁב	נוֹשַׁב	הִתְיַשֵּׁב
3 ms impf.	יְיַשֵּׁב	יְיֻשַּׁב	יוֹשִׁיב	יוּשַׁב	יִוָּשֵׁב	יִתְיַשֵּׁב
2 ms impv.	יַשֵּׁב	–	הוֹשֵׁב	–	הִוָּשֵׁב	הִתְיַשֵּׁב
participles	מְיַשֵּׁב	מְיֻשָּׁב	מוֹשִׁיב	מוּשָׁב	נוֹשָׁב	מִתְיַשֵּׁב

The Pe Waw Verb in the Qal stem

As in the Pe Nun verb, the true Pe Waw verb has three classes in the Qal. Again these differ among themselves only in the infinitive construct, imperfect, and imperative. The verbs characterized by a holem after the second radical in imperfect and imperative are quite unimportant. The Pathah statives or Class II verbs are in the majority, but there are nine verbs most of which are very important forming Class III. These are characterized by a Sere under the second radical of the imperfect and imperative. In particular:

Class I is very like קָטַל except that often the Yodh is assimilated in the imperfect exactly as if

---

(1) It may be mentioned here that the Hiriq of the preformative in the Hiphil perfect, Niphal perfect and participle, and imperfect Qal; also the Hiriq under the first radical of the Piel perfect is a secondary development from an original Pathah. Cf. the discussion of the origin of the פ"י forms in Bergstrasser, Pt.2, p 130.

it were a Nun. The peculiar circumstance is that this class is practically confined to verbs with Sadhe for the second radical. One of the few examples is יָצַק "pour."

Class II Pe Waw is very much like the corresponding Pe Nun class. The second radical in the imperfect and imperative has the similar pathah. The weak Yodh is lost, usually, in the imperative. In the infinitive construct also, the Yodh is lost and a segholate form results. In the imperfect, the Yodh as a vowel letter quiesces making the vowel of the preformative long.

Class III, like נָתַן , has the Sere with the second radical of the imperfect and imperative. The Yodh is lost again in the infinitive construct and a segholate form results. Since, however, there is no final Nun as in נָתַן to complicate the picture, a true segholate form is found, לֶדֶת ,from יָלַד ,except where some complication arises as in the case of יָצָא where the quiescing of the final Aleph makes the form צֵאת , very much like תֵּת . In the imperative the Yodh is simply dropped. In the imperfect, the Yodh is this time dropped completely and a Sere is found after the preformative which may at least be remembered by its beautifully matching the Sere of the second syllable.

A comparative paradigm of פ"נ and פ"ו verbs in the Qal is as follows:

	פ"נ Cl.I	פ"ו Cl.I	Cl. II	Cl. II	Cl.III	Cl.III
Inf.con.	נְפֹל	צֶקֶת	גֶּשֶׁת	רֶשֶׁת	תֵּת	שֶׁבֶת
Impf.2 ms	תִּפֹּל	תִּצֹּק	תִּגַּשׁ	תִּירַשׁ	תִּתֵּן	תֵּשֵׁב
2 fs	תִּפְּלִי	תִּצְּקִי	תִּגְּשִׁי	תִּירְשִׁי	תִּתְּנִי	תֵּשְׁבִי
2 fp	תִּפֹּלְנָה	תִּצֹּקְנָה	תִּגַּשְׁנָה	תִּירַשְׁנָה	תִּתֵּנָּה	תֵּשַׁבְנָה
Impv.2 ms	נְפֹל	יְצֹק	גַּשׁ	רֵשׁ	תֵּן	שֵׁב
2 fs	נִפְלִי	יִצְקִי	גְּשִׁי	רְשִׁי	תְּנִי	שְׁבִי
2 fp	נְפֹלְנָה	יְצֹקְנָה	גַּשְׁנָה	רַשְׁנָה	תֵּנָּה	שֵׁבְנָה

It should be mentioned that the verb הָלַךְ acts just like a Pe Waw verb, Class III, except in the Qal perfect, infinitive absolute and participles where the He is initial. In the Piel, Pual, and Hithpael the He is retained also, but the Hiphil is הוֹלִיךְ , יוֹלִיךְ ,etc.

Pe Yodh Verbs

A very few verbs, notably יָטַב "be good,(related to טוֹב) and יָנַק "suck," had originally a Yodh, not Waw in the first position. These verbs act exactly like the Pe Waw verbs we have studied except that throughout the Hiphil they do not have a Holem after the preformative, but instead a Sere-Yodh, e.g.: 3 ms. perfect Hiphil הֵיטִיב , 3 ms. imperfect Hiphil וַיֵּיטִיב .

Vocabulary

יָרֵא fear,reverence (Cl.II)

יָרַד go down (Cl.III, with Waw cons. וַיֵּרֶד)

יָרַשׁ possess,inherit(Q) dispossess (H); (Cl.II)

יָצָא go out (Cl.III)

יָטַב be good (Q) do good(H) (Cl.II, Pe Yodh)

הָלַךְ go(Q)march (P),lead(H) (like Cl.III Pe Waw)

יָלַד bear a child (Cl.III with Waw cons. וַיֵּלֶד)

יָשַׁב sit, dwell (Cl.III note וַיֵּשֶׁב)

יָדַע know (Q),make known (H); (Cl.III,impf. יֵדַע ,inf.con. דֵּעַ)

יָסַף add (Q and H) esp.with following verb means "do again." (Cl.III)

Exercises

A. Write יָרַשׁ and יָלַד in the entire Qal stem.
B. Do exercise B p.47 first for יָרַשׁ then for יָשַׁב .
C. Translate the following forms then parse them:

1. הוֹלַדְתִּי 2. וַתֵּרֶד 3. צְאִי 4. הוֹדִיעַ 5. וַיֵּלֶךְ 6. שְׁבָנָה

7. חוֹסֵף 8. נוּרַשׁ 9. שֶׁבֶת 10. נֵיטִיב 11. נוֹרָא 12. יְדַע

13. מַלְכָּה 14. וְרָשְׁנָה 15. צֵאת

D. Translate the following using lexicon as necessary:

1. וַיֵּצֵא בַשָּׂדֶה וְהוּא יֹשֵׁב בְּאֶרֶץ הַנֶּגֶב וַיִּשָּׂא(1)אֶת־הָעֵינַיִם וַיַּרְא אֶת־הֶעָבֶד עַל גָּמָל: 2. וְרִבְקָה יֹשֶׁבֶת עַל גָּמָל וַתִּפֹּל מֵעַל הַגָּמָל וַתֹּאמֶר אֶל־עֶבֶד מִי הָאִישׁ הַהֹלֵךְ בַּשָּׂדֶה: 3. וַיַּעַן הָעֶבֶד הוּא יִצְחָק וַיִּקַּח יִצְחָק אֶת־רִבְקָה לְאִשָּׁה: 4. וַיּוֹסֶף אַבְרָהָם וַיִּקַּח אִשָּׁה וַתֵּלֶד בֵּן וַיּוֹלֶד הַבֵּן בָּנִים וּבָנוֹת: 5. וַתֵּלֶד רִבְקָה אֶת־יַעֲקֹב וְאֶת־עֵשָׂו וַיִּגְדָּלוּ: 6. וְעָשׂוּ אִישׁ יֹדֵעַ צַיִד אִישׁ הַשָּׂדֶה וְיַעֲקֹב אִישׁ יֹשֵׁב אֹהָלִים: 7. וַיִּתֵּן יַעֲקֹב לְעֵשָׂו לֶחֶם וַיֹּאכַל עֵשָׂו וַיֵּלֶךְ: 8. וַיִּירַשׁ יַעֲקֹב אֶת בְּכֹרַת עֵשָׂו:

___

(1) Dual of עַיִן 'pair of eyes."

9. וַיִּירָא יַעֲקֹב לְדַבֵּר אֶל הָאָב כִּי לֹא יֵשֵׁב וְהָאִם יְדַעַת אֶת־הֶעָשׂוּי:

10. וַיֵּצֵא יַעֲקֹב וַיֵּרֶד לַצֹּאן וַיִּקַּח צֹאן וַיֹּסֶף לֶכֶת אֶל־אֹהֶל הָאָב:

11. וַיִּירָא וַיֹּאמֶר רִבְקָה אֵיטִיב אֶת־הַדָּבָר בְּעֵינֵי הָאָב:

12. וַיֹּאמֶר עֵשָׂו בַּלֵּב אֶקְטֹל אֶת־הָאָח:

13. וַיֻּגַּד לְרִבְקָה אֶת־דִּבְרֵי עֵשָׂו וַתֹּאמֶר לְיַעֲקֹב לֶךְ־לְךָ אֶל לָבָן:

14. וַיֵּצֵא וַיֵּלֶךְ אֶל בֵּית־אֵל:

15. וַיֹּאמֶר הַמָּקוֹם נוֹרָא הוּא שַׁעַר הַשָּׁמָיִם:

E. Translate into Hebrew:
1. The man will be afraid before the king. 2. She will cause the men to go down in order to possess the land and to dwell there. 3. And Abraham added to take wives and they bore sons and they begot sons and daughters. 4. And the king commanded saying, "Do good to the man because he is the son of the king." 5. And the man went out and the wicked one knew that he had gone out.

Lesson 14   The Pronoun Suffixes

The personal pronouns in the possessive or objective cases do not stand alone, but consist of suffixes attached to nouns, verbs, and prepositions. The suffixes are a little different when attached to verbs and the rules for attachment are quite involved. The rules for attachment to the noun are somewhat simpler, but still difficult in detail. Fortunately, in translation it is not so necessary to know how the suffix is attached, but only which suffix appears. It is therefore very important to know the meanings of the various suffixes so that they can be recognized rapidly and accurately. The same pro – nominal suffixes which are possessive when attached to nouns are used as objective pronouns when applied to pre-positions or the sign of the accusative אֵת . They are as follows:

Singular		Plural	
my, me	י	our, us	נוּ
thy (m),thee	ךָ	your (m),you	כֶם
thy (f),thee	ךְ	your (f),you	כֶן
his, him	וֹ (הוּ)	their (m), them	ם ַ (הֶם)
her	הָ (ָהּ)	their (f), them	ן ַ (הֶן)

In the above list the forms in parentheses are those preferred if the noun or preposition ends in a vowel. Rarely a third form הָ will be found for the 3 ms. suffix "his." This is a hybrid form using the consonant ה of the older הו and the vowel of וֹ . A rare alternative form מוֹ for the 3 mp. suffix "their"(m) is also found, chiefly in poetry. It is probably an archaism.

In an introductory grammar we can not consider the various classes of nouns with the vowel changes to be expected in each case upon addition of these suffixes. Gesenius' grammar lists (pp 227 to 241) 12 main classes of nouns with 55 subclasses depending upon what the original form of the noun was. To follow out this study would be valuable, but would require much time and some knowledge of the cognate languages and of historical Hebrew grammar. Gesenius gives a briefer and very valuable discussion on p 260f of the principles and general character of vowel changes in nouns upon inflection. Complete paradigms of typical masculine, feminine, and irregular nouns with full discussion follow on pp 262 to 284.

It is enough for our purposes, generally, to disregard these vowel changes as not affecting the meaning of the words nor being the best indication of their form. Our method is insufficient for Hebrew composition but is adequate for beginners translating from Hebrew into English and for much exegetical study.

The fact is that a word like דָּבָר is accented on the ultima. In the plural or with an ending like that found in דְּבָרָיו the accent moves forward one syllable as shown. With a heavy or "grave" suffix (כֶם הֶן כֶן and הֶן) the accent or "tone" moves forward two places: דִּבְרֵיהֶם. This situation often resembles that of the const. state where the force of the accent is carried over to the following word. Obviously this shift of accent will cause considerable modification of the vowels, but these changes do not affect either the meaning or recognizability of the form and therefore can be disregarded to a certain extent by the beginner.

Rather, the student should learn to note the consonants of the noun, which indicate its meaning; secondly the person, number, and gender of the suffixed pronoun; and thirdly the ending of the noun to which the pronoun is attached, which will show the number and gender of the noun.

Reflection will show that the genitive pronoun suffixes are attached to nouns in the construct state. As we say "horse of Abraham," we may also say "horse of him" except that "him" is attached directly to its noun. Thus for the noun שָׁנָה "year," the form to which suffixes are attached is שְׁנַת . For mp. nouns like סוּסִים , the form used with suffixes is סוּסֵי . For fp. nouns such as עוֹלוֹת the form used with suffixes is עוֹלוֹת . The vowels of the body of the noun may change in several ways, but the key to the gender and number *of the noun* is in the ending of the noun just before the suffix. No ending indicates a ms. noun, the ending -ָת- indicates fs., the ending - ֵי - indicates mp., and - וֹת -(more usually וֹתֵי by analogy to the mp.) indicates fp.

Thus דִּבְרֵיהֶם is "their (m) words" no matter what its vowels. מַלְכָּתִי can be recognized as "my queen" without the vowels. Also חַרְבוֹתָם also spelled חַרְבוֹתֵיהֶם is "their (m) swords" regardless of what its proper vowels are. The vowels will differ with heavy and light suffixes just as they usually differ with abs. and const. state, but the noun can be analyzed apart from the vowels by observing (1) the consonants of the noun, (2) the suffix, and (3) the ending of the noun; whether: none (ms.), -ָת- (fs.), - ֵי- (mp.), or -וֹתֵי- (or -וֹת-) (fp.). These remarks only refer to the form of the noun, for there are many feminine nouns which are masculine in form and therefore lack the -ָת- ending before suffixes. As a rule, these feminine nouns masculine in form change to a feminine form in the plural.

Like the sufformatives of the perfect of verbs, these suffixes are divided into heavy endings (listed above) and light endings (all the rest). All these endings attract the accent, but the heavy or "grave" endings cause more radical alteration of the vowels of the root form because they attract the accent more decidedly to the ultima. It will be seen that all the light suffixes affect the tone to the same degree and therefore all such forms will be similar except for the suffix. Likewise all forms bearing the grave suffix will be similar except for the ending. In order to know a noun completely it is necessary to know the absolute and construct, singular and plural and the singular and plural forms with grave and with light suffixes. These eight forms are given for many typical nouns in Ges. pp 264, 277, and 282.

A caution should be expressed for parsing feminine nouns. Remember that the fs. absolute state ends in ־הָ and therefore if the noun in question has the ending -ָת- or -וֹתֶי־ before suffixes, these construct endings should be replaced by the הָ of the fs. absolute before the noun is looked up in a vocabulary. Thus שְׁנָתוֹ should be looked up under שָׁנָה from the root שָׁנָה and עֹלוֹתֵיכֶם should be looked up under עֹלָה from the root עָלָה .

Since pronouns are definite, a noun in the construct state before a suffixed pronoun is also definite per se, and will never take the article. Thus "my good servant" is: עַבְדִּי הַטּוֹב .

As remarked above, these pronouns can be attached to the sign of the accusative אֵת in which case they become objective. The form of the particle is then usually -אֹת . Thus "he killed him" is קָטַל אֹתוֹ .

Paradigm of Pronoun Suffixes in Various Forms

	with reg. sing. noun ending in consonant	with reg. pl. noun in masc. or feminine	attached to הֶקָּה form חֶקַּת	attached to סוּסִים form סוּסֵי	with לְ (1)
my	ִ י (2)	ַ י (2)	חֶקָּתִי	סוּסַי	לִי
thy (m)	ךָ	יךָ	חֶקָּתְךָ	סוּסֶיךָ	לְךָ
thy (f)	ךְ	יִךְ	חֶקָּתֵךְ	סוּסַיִךְ	לָךְ
his	וֹ	יו	חֶקָּתוֹ	סוּסָיו	לוֹ
her	הָ	יהָ	חֶקָּתָהּ	סוּסֶיהָ	לָהּ
our	נוּ	ינוּ	חֶקָּתֵנוּ	סוּסֵינוּ	לָנוּ
your (m)	כֶם	יכֶם	חֶקַּתְכֶם	סוּסֵיכֶם	לָכֶם
your (f)	כֶן	יכֶן	חֶקַּתְכֶן	סוּסֵיכֶן	לָכֶן
their (m)	ם	יהֶם	חֶקָּתָם	סוּסֵיהֶם	לָהֶם
their (f)	ן	יהֶן	חֶקָּתָן	סוּסֵיהֶן	לָהֶן

Irregular nouns act similarly. In general, those whose construct ends in a vowel take the suffixes as listed on p. 52. Those ending in a consonant take forms as in the first column above. Cf. Ges. p. 282ff for complete details.

(1) כְּ before light suffixes becomes - כָּמוֹ

(2) Note this ' is the ' of the m. pl. const. or the ' on the f. pl. const. added by analogy - not a part of suffix.

Vocabulary

בֶּגֶד garment

שָׂדֶה field (const. שְׂדֵה, pl. שָׂדוֹת suffixes add to שְׂדֹ־)

נַעַר boy (f. נַעֲרָה girl)

פֶּה mouth (const. פִּי)

אַחַר after (pl. אַחֲרֵי with and without suffixes)

וַיְהִי and it came to pass

מִי who?

עַל, אֶל with suffixes עָלַי־, אֵלַי־ like pl. nouns

אֲשֶׁר who, which, that; he who, that which, Rel. particle

מִן with suffixes מִמְּ־ , or מִמֶּנְ־ (by reduplication)

Exercises

A. Write from memory בְּ with all the pronoun suffixes, also סוּס and חָקוֹת (form חָקוֹתִי־) with each suffix.
B. Translate the following and give the absolute state of each:

1. בָּנֵינוּ 2. פִּיהוּ 3. שָׂדְךָ 4. נַעֲרָה 5. אִמּוֹתָם 6. מַעֲשָׂיו

7. נַעֲרוֹתַיִךְ 8. מִצְוָתִי 9. צֹאנְכֶם 10. אֲבִיהֶן

C. Write in Hebrew using only the vowels of the suffix:
1. our garments 2. your (m) fields 3. from me 4. her girls 5. thy (m) mouth 6. their (f) boy 7. their (m) deeds 8. his burnt offering 9. thy (f) sheep 10. to him

D. Translate using lexicon and practice silent reading:

1. וַתֹּאמֶר רוּת אֶל־אֲשֶׁר תֵּלְכִי אֵלֵךְ עַמֵּךְ עַמִּי וֵאלֹהַיִךְ אֱלֹהָי:

2. בַּאֲשֶׁר תִּקָּבְרִי אֶקָּבֵר: 3. כֹּה יַעֲשֶׂה יְהוָה לִי וְכֹה יֹסִיף כִּי אֶעֱבֹר מֵאַחֲרַיִךְ: 4. וַתֵּרֶא כִּי הָלוֹךְ תֵּלֵךְ עִמָּהּ וַתֶּחְדַּל לְדַבֵּר אֵלֶיהָ: 5. וַתֵּלַכְנָה אֶל בֵּית לֶחֶם וַיְהִי כָּל הָעָם יֹצְאִים אֵלֶיהָ: 6. וַתֹּאמֶר לָנָשִׁים הַתִּקְרֶאנָה לִי נָעֳמִי וַיהוָה עָנָה בִי:

7. וּלְנָעֳמִי מוֹדָע לְאִישָׁהּ אִישׁ גָּדוֹל וּשְׁמוֹ בֹּעַז: 8. וַתֹּאמֶר רוּת אֵלֶיהָ אֵלֶךְ לַשָּׂדוּ לָקַחַת לֶחֶם וַתֹּאמֶר לָהּ לְכִי בִתִּי: 9. וַתֵּלֶךְ וַתְּלַקֵּט בְּשָׂדֶה בֹעַז בְּכָל יוֹם: 10. וַיֵּצֵא בֹעַז מִבֵּית לֶחֶם לַשָּׂדוֹת וַיֹּאמֶר לְנַעֲרָיו יְהוָה עִמָּכֶם וַיַּעֲנוּ לוֹ יְבָרֶךְ אֹתְךָ יְהוָה: 11. וַיֹּאמֶר בֹּעַז לְנַעֲרוֹ מִי הַנַּעֲרָה הַמְלַקֵּטָה בַּשָּׂדֶה 12. וַיַּעַן הַנַּעַר וַיֹּאמֶר הִיא רוּת אֲשֶׁר עָבְרָה עִם נָעֳמִי מִשְּׂדֵי מוֹאָב: 13. וַיֹּאמֶר אֶל־רוּת הֲלֹא שָׁמַעַתְּ בִּתִּי לֹא־תַעֲבוּרִי מִשָּׂדִי: 14. וְכֹה תִדְבָּקִי עִם־נַעֲרֹתַי וְעֵינַיִךְ בַּשָּׂדֶה אֲשֶׁר יִקְצֹרוּ:

Lesson 15   The Syllable, Accent, and Vowel Change

The Syllable

In Hebrew every syllable begins with a consonant, except the conjunction when it takes the form וּ .
Syllables are of two main classes, open and closed. Open
syllables are those ending with a vowel קָ ֹ Some open
syllables are often called half open or artificially o-
pened, as בְּקַטֵל for בְּקַטֵּל , or יַעֲמִיד for יַעֲמִיד . Such
are also the first syllables of the segholates לֶד - מַ .
Closed syllables are those ending with a consonant: מִן .
Closed syllables ending with the first of a doubled letter are often called sharpened קַטֵּל . A very few syllables end in two consonants and are called doubly closed
קָטַלְתְּ - קְ . A consonant with vocal shewa under it does not
count in syllable division but is considered as going with
the following syllable. Quiescent letters also are not
counted, thus לֹא is an open syllable.

Accent

Every word not joined to another bears an accent, or tone as it is often called. In the Hebrew Bible
this accent is marked by any one of about 50 small signs
such as ̈ ̣ ̣ ֧ etc. These signs serve a double purpose,
first to mark the accent and second to indicate punctua-
tion. These signs were adopted by the Jews during the
Middle Ages to assist in standardizing the public reading of the Scripture and their function was thus to help
in the liturgy. The meanings of the accent marks differ
in the poetical books of Job, Psalms, and Proverbs. For
our purposes we may disregard most of them and shall indicate the accent thus ˋ when it is marked.

The accent usually stands on the ultima, sometimes on the penult. It can never go back further though
a countertone or secondary accent frequently stands earlier in the word. Places where the accent does not stand
on the ultima are chiefly 1) light verbal sufformatives
(the heavy forms כֶם and כֶן carry the tone), 2) segholate
nouns - not only מֶלֶךְ but such obscured segholates as בַּיִת
בֹּקֶר סֵפֶר etc. These nouns were originally of the form
malku. They became mono-syllabic when the final short
vowel (a case ending) was lost. The vowel now found between the last two letters is a helping vowel or "anaptyctic" vowel, usually a seghol, which naturally could
not bear the accent,   3) the Waw cons. with some forms
of the impf. without endings (cf. pp. 34 and 39), and
4) special cases where the rhythm of the sentence
causes changes in individual words.

Two or more words joined by maqqeph (‑) make one accent unit. A construct state has no accent, or at least a very weak one which does not affect the vocalization.

Of the small signs marking the accent, two are important: 1) the Athnah (∧) which marks the principal stop in the logical middle of every verse. 2) The Metheg (╷). The metheg is a sign meaning "notice! do not slur this vowel!" Its most frequent use is to mark the count-ertone which, when found, is usually in the second open syllable before the tone, thus: הָאָדָם . Another important use is to emphasize a long vowel followed by vocal shewa followed by the tone syllable, thus: קָמְלָה .

Vowel Change

It will perhaps be of more value to the beginner to observe first which vowels do not change. Three classes may be given: a) Those vowels usually written with accompanying vowel letters (as ִי . ֵי ֹ ו ֻ ו) for the most part remain unchanged in inflection. b) Vowels arising by compensatory heightening are unchangeable. c) Short vowels in closed syllables not final are usually unchangeable. Thus הִקְטִיל and הִקְטִילוּ , הָעֳבֵד and הָעֳבָדִים , מִשְׁפָּט and מִשְׁפָּטִים .

The vowels which change most frequently are the five short vowels _ , ֹ , ֶ , ֱ , ֳ (qames hatuph), and the three vowels often called "tone long" : ָ , ֵ , and ֹ . These latter are often heightened from the corresponding short vowels. When the influence that raised them is gone, they may revert to the short vowel or may drop all the way to a shewa. Rules governing these changes are as follows:

1) The tone long vowels arise in closed syllables under the influence of the accent (tone lengthening) except that this does not usually occur in verbs, e.g. דָּבָר but קָטַל .

2) The tone long vowels, especially the qames, arise in an open syllable just before the tone (pre-tone lengthening) except in verb forms with vocalic sufformatives, e.g. דְּבָרִים but קָמְלוּ (not קָמְלוּ).

3) These vowels all drop to a half vowel when they would be left in an open syllable two places from the accent, unless they are maintained by a secondary accent, e.g. קָמְלָה but קָמְלוּ .

Pausal Forms

In addition to the above system there is a lengthening of forms occurring at the end and middle of verses and marked by special accent. The accent on the

final word (called Silluq) and the verse divider, Athnah
(see above) cause the accented vowels in the words concerned to be lengthened. A short vowel will lengthen to
the corresponding tone long vowel. A vocal shewa will
often be restored to its original short vowel and then
lengthened to the tone long counterpart. A few other accents besides the Silluq and Athnah will sometimes also
cause pausal lengthening but the Masoretic text usually
indicates these cases by a special footnote.

The operation of the above rules can often be
observed by the beginner, but in order to apply them ful-
ly it is necessary to know the origin of many particular
forms which frequently can only be learned by comparison
with other Semitic languages. Therefore a beginner can
not always predict vowel changes. He can notice that a
Pathah often changes to Qames and vice versa with gain or
loss of the tone; also a Hiriq, Sere, and Seghol change
among themselves; also a Holem, Qibbus, and Qames Hatuph
change into each other under certain conditions. Heterogeneous vowels do not interchange under the influence of
the tone. Beyond these simple rules the student can a-
wait the study of an advanced grammar.

To sum up our study, we may say that the usual
Hebrew word is built around the tone syllable. The vowel of this syllable will be long except in verb forms.
Toneless closed syllables will have short vowels. The
syllable just before the tone, if open, has a long vowel. If there were another open syllable two places removed from the tone, the tendency would be for that vowel
to drop to a vocal shewa - or it could bear the countertone and take a Metheg. When the accent is shifted there
will be consequent alteration of the vowels to conform
to the above rules. Certain vowels, however, will not
be changed, according to rules a,b, and c above.

Vocabulary

שָׁכַם   rise early (H)

קָרָא   call, proclaim

קָרָה or קָרָא encounter,
        befall, meet

שָׂנֵא   hate

נָגַע   touch, strike (Q)
        reach, arrive (H)

שָׁתָה   drink

מַדּוּעַ   wherefore?

אֵת   with (as prep.) when used
      with suff. is אִתִּי, אִתּוֹ

רַק   only, surely

כֵּן   so, thus (adv.)
       עַל־כֵּן   therefore

בֵּין   between (used with pro.
        suffixes)

אִם   hypoth. part. if. After oath
emph. neg. Also interr. part. if, or

Exercises

A. Mark the accent on the following words, noting the unchangeable vowels and the effects of accent shift:

1. הַדָּבָר 2. הַדְּבָרִים 3. דְּבָרֵי 4. שְׁמַרְתֶּם 5. הִשְׁמַרְתֶּם 6. קָטוּל

7. קְטוּלָה 8. יַקְטִיל 9. וַיַּקְטִיל 10. וַיִּקְטְלוּ 11. הָעֹבְדִים

12. הָעֶבֶד 13. מִשְׁפָּט 14. מִשְׁפָּט 15. מִשְׁפָּטִים

B. Parse the following verbs and nouns:

1. הַפִּיל 2. נוֹרָא 3. וַיֵּלֶךְ 4. תִּתְּנָה 5. מוֹצֵאת 6. הָלוֹךְ

7. נֶשֶׁת 8. רֶשֶׁת 9. דַּע 10. זְכַרְתֶּם 11. לְאָבִיךְ 12. אִשְׁתְּךָ

13. בְּמִצְוָתְךָ 14. בָּתֵּיהֶם 15. וַעֲוֺנֵינוּ

C. Translate, with lexicon, noting the effects of accent:

1. וַיִּבֶן שָׁם מִזְבֵּחַ וַיִּקְרָא בְּשֵׁם יְהוָה *וַיֵּט־שָׁם אָהֳלוֹ וַיִּכְרוּ־
שָׁם עַבְדֵי־יִצְחָק בְּאֵר: 2. וַאֲבִימֶלֶךְ הָלַךְ אֵלָיו מִגְּרָר וַאֲחֻזַּת
מֵרֵעֵהוּ וּפִיכֹל שַׂר־צְבָאוֹ: 3. וַיֹּאמֶר אֲלֵהֶם יִצְחָק מַדּוּעַ
**בָּאתֶם אֵלָי וְאַתֶּם שְׂנֵאתֶם אֹתִי **וַתְּשַׁלְּחוּנִי מֵאִתְּכֶם:
4. וַיֹּאמְרוּ רָאוֹ רָאִינוּ כִּי־הָיָה יְהוָה עִמָּךְ וַנֹּאמֶר תְּהִי
אָלָה בֵּינֵינוּ וּבֵינֶךָ ***וְנִכְרְתָה בְּרִית עִמָּךְ: 5. אִם־תַּעֲשֵׂה
עִמָּנוּ רָעָה כַּאֲשֶׁר לֹא **נְגַעֲנוּךָ וְכַאֲשֶׁר עָשִׂינוּ עִמְּךָ רַק־
טוֹב **וַנְּשַׁלֵּחֲךָ בְּשָׁלוֹם אַתָּה עַתָּה בָּרוּךְ יְהוָה: 6. וַיַּעַשׂ
לָהֶם מִשְׁתֶּה וַיֹּאכְלוּ וַיִּשְׁתּוּ: 7. וַיַּשְׁכִּימוּ בַבֹּקֶר וַיִּשָּׁבְעוּ אִישׁ
לְאָחִיו **וַיְשַׁלְּחֵם יִצְחָק וַיֵּלְכוּ מֵאִתּוֹ בְּשָׁלֹם: 8. וַיְהִי בַּיּוֹם
הַהוּא וַיָּבֹאוּ עַבְדֵי יִצְחָק וַיַּגִּדוּ לוֹ עַל־דִּבְר הַבְּאֵר אֲשֶׁר חָפָרוּ:

*Qal of נָטָה **Qal of בּוֹא **pronoun on verb ***cohortative הָ meaning "let us."

Lesson 16 The Ayin Waw Verb

The fourth class of irregular verb, the Ayin-
Waw is characterized by a weakness in the middle or Ayin
position. The Waw in the middle of the root either becomes a vowel letter or is completely lost leaving a monosyllabic root. To compensate for this loss, the vowel of
the preformative is usually longer, if there be a preformative. The Hophal, Hiphil, and Niphal stems are the
easiest and may be studied first.

In the Hophal, the middle Waw drops out completely leaving radicals 1 & 3 to act just like radicals 2 & 3
of the strong verb. In short, the last part of the verb-
what may be called the root syllable -will look exactly
like the corresponding syllable of the regular verb.   The
Qames Hatuph of the preformative syllable of the regular
verb is now lengthened as a long vowel in an open pretone syllable to make a Shureq throughout. Thus for קוּם
"rise" characteristic forms are: הוּקְמָתִי, וּיּוּקְמוּ, מוּקָם.

In the Hiphil, likewise, the middle Waw drops
out leaving a monosyllabic root syllable. Again radicals 1 & 3 act just like radicals 2 & 3 of the regular
verb. The vowel under the preformative, being in an open
pretone syllable is lengthened and becomes a Sere in pf.
and ptc. and a Qames everywhere else. This characteristic
of the Hiphil of Ayin-Waw verbs is very important and
must be kept in mind. The Hiphil Ayin-Waw has a Sere under the preformative in the pf. and ptc. and Qames under
the preformative in inf., impf., and impv. The last part
of the verb looks quite regular being like the root syllable of the regular verb. Typical forms are: הֵקִימוּ ,
הָקִים , יָקִים , יָקִימוּ , הָקֵם , מֵקִים .

The Niphal stem is easy to recognize because it
retains the Waw throughout. Any verb which has the Waw
between two strong root consonants is practically certain
to be Ayin-Waw and either Niphal or Qal. The vowels of
the preformative Niphal are Qames in pf. and ptc.(where
the vowel must be long in an open pretone syllable) and
Hiriq everywhere else with the first radical doubled. The
Qames usually under the doubled first radical in the inf.
impf. and impv. is omitted in view of the Waw immediately
following. Typical forms are: נָקוֹם, הֵקּוֹם, יִקּוֹם, יִקּוֹמוּ.

One exception to the above rules must be noted.
The pf. Hiphil and Niphal with consonantal suformatives
is modified. In the Hiphil pf. before consonantal sufformatives, a helping vowel, Holem, is inserted just before the suformative. In consequence, the vowel of the
preformative is dropped and becomes Hateph Pathah under
the laryngeal He. Thus הֵקִים with consonantal sufformatives is: הֲקִימוֹתִי , הֲקִימוֹנוּ , etc. The Niphal pf. before consonantal sufformatives also adds the helping
vowel, Holem, and in consequence drops the vowel of the
preformative to shewa. A slight additional change is made
in the central Waw, which becomes Shureq before light
sufformatives and Holem before grave. Thus נָקוֹם with
cons. suff. is: נְקוּמוֹתִי, נְקוּמוֹתָ, נְקוּמוֹת, נְקוּמוֹנוּ, נְקוּמוֹתֶם

The Qal stem in the Ayin-Waw verbs is, as usual,
a bit more confusing than the derived stems. Yet the principle is the familiar one that the root syllable is monosyllabic and the vowel under the preformative is pretone
long, if there be a preformative. In the pf. the middle
radical drops out entirely and the vowel is simply Qames
changing to Pathah before consonantal sufformatives. In
a few verbs, some of the statives, such as מוּת, the vowel
is Sere changing to Pathah, thus: מֵת מֵתָה מַתָּ מַתְּ
מַתִּי . In the impf. the middle Waw is retained as
a Shureq and the vowel of the preformative is Qames. This
Qames is a pretone lengthening from the original Pathah
which formerly stood in this position in the active verbs
(see notes pp. 49 and 33). It appears that stative verbs
originally had a Hiriq in this position and some of them
show pretone lengthening to a Sere, thus: אָקוּם יְקוּמִי
יָקוּם but יֵבוֹשׁ . There is a slight exception with the
two consonantal sufformatives of the plural. Sometimes
there is a helping vowel ִי inserted just before the sufformative, and sometimes the Shureq changes to Holem,
thus: תְּקוּמֶינָה or תְּקֹמְנָה . Much confusion results because
of the similarity of the impf. Qal and the impf. Hiphil
of these verbs. Both have the Qames under the preformative. But the Qal has an U-class vowel in the middle whereas
the Hiphil has an I-class vowel. The impv. Qal is just
like the impf. with the preformative dropped. The inf.
(in these verbs the inf. const. is the form cited in the
lexicon) and the participles Qal had better be learned
by rote rather than by rule. Key form of the stems so
far studied are as follows:

	Qal	Hiphil	Hophal	Niphal
pf. 3 ms.	קָם	הֵקִים	הוּקַם	נָקוֹם
3 cp.	קָמוּ	הֵקִימוּ	הוּקְמוּ	נָקוֹמוּ
1 cp.	קַמְנוּ	הֲקִימוֹנוּ	הוּקַמְנוּ	נְקוּמוֹנוּ
2 mp.	קַמְתֶּם	הֲקִימוֹתֶם	הוּקַמְתֶּם	נְקֻמוֹתֶם
inf. abs.	קוֹם	הָקֵם	הוּקֵם	הִקּוֹם
inf. const.	קוּם	הָקִים	הוּקַם	(or נָקוֹם) הִקּוֹם
impf. 2 ms.	תָּקוּם	תָּקִים	תּוּקַם	תִּקּוֹם
2 fs.	תָּקוּמִי	תָּקִימִי	תּוּקְמִי	תִּקּוֹמִי
2 fp.	תְּקֻמֶנָה (or תְּקוּמֶינָה)	תְּקִמֶינָה (or תְּקֵמְנָה)	תּוּקַמְנָה	תִּקּוֹמְנָה
part. act. קָם pas. קוּם	מֵקִים	מוּקַם	נָקוֹם

Apocopation of Ayin-Waw Verbs

The Ayin-Waw verb suffers apocopation only in the Qal and Hiphil. Again the forms with sufformatives, also the first persons, are not affected. In the Qal with a Waw cons. the middle vowel, Shureq, is dropped to Qames Hatuph, thus: יָקוּם becomes וַיָּקָם . In the Hiphil, the middle vowel, Hiriq, is dropped to a Seghol, thus יָקִים becomes וַיָּקֶם . It is to be noted that the apocopated forms of the Qal and Hiphil are quite similar and often cause confusion. But still it may be remembered that the Qal has the U-class vowel in the middle and the Hiphil has the I-class.

Vocabulary

קוּם	rise, stand (Talitha Cumi-maid arise. cf. מָקוֹם -standing place)	נֶגַע	stroke, plague (cf נָגַע)
סוּר	turn aside	הָרַג	kill, slay
מוּת	die (Q) kill (H)	הָיָה	come to pass, become, be (3 ms Q with Waw וַיְהִי)
רוּם	be high (cf Ramoth Gilead)	חָיָה	live (Q) preserve alive (P or H)
שׁוּב	turn back, return (cf Shear-yashub Is.7:3)	מָוֶת	death (cf מוּת)
גּוּר	sojourn (cf Gershom - sojourner)	לַיְלָה	night (m) const: לֵיל pl. לֵילוֹת
בּוּן	establish (H) be established (N)	גּוֹי	nation, pl. גּוֹיִם (mostly of heathen nations)
בּוּשׁ	be ashamed (keeps וֹ in Q. cf Ishbosheth)	תֹּם	integrity. (const. תָּם with suf. תֻּמִּי from תֹּמֶם)
בּוֹא	enter, go in (impf. Q יָבוֹא , impv. בּוֹא)	כַּף	flat of hand or foot, palm (with suf. כַּפִּי)
חָטָא	sin (Q) purify with an offering (P)	הִנֵּה , הֵן behold! (with suf. הִנְנִי behold I, הִנָּךְ)
נָא	I pray (after verbs almost like "please")	עִמָּדִי	with (form of עִם used with suf. ׳.) 'with me"

Exercises

A. Write the complete Qal, Hiphil, and Niphal of שׁוּב
B. Parse the following forms:

1. נְבוֹנוֹתָ   2. הָרִים   3. וַיָּבוֹאוּ   4. פָּמַחְתָּה   5. סָר   6. וַיִּגֶּר

7. וַתֵּשֶׁב   8. וַיֵּשֶׁב   9. בָּאתְ   10. הֲבִנוֹתִי   11. בּוֹשְׁנוּ   12. קוּמִי

13. אֶחְיֶה   14. חְטְאוּ   15. לָלֶדֶת   16. הוּשַׁבְתֶּם   17. נְבוֹנֹת

18. וַיַּעַל   19. תֵּבוֹשׁוּ   20. מֵתִין   21. נַעֲשִׂינוּ   22. תָּשֹׁבוֹת

23. בָּבוֹא   24. סֹרְנָה   25. רְשִׁי

C. Translate 2 Sam. 6:1-11. Verse 5 may be omitted. Note the forms וַיַּבְּהוּ and וַיִּשָּׂהוּ from נָבָה and נָשָׂא with the 3 ms. pronoun suffix.

Lesson 17   Ayin-Waw Verb (cont.)   Other Moods of Verbs

Intensive Stems of Ayin-Waw Verbs

The Piel, Pual, and Hithpael are seldom used in these verbs. When they are used, the middle radical is changed to Yodh and doubled in the usual manner, thus: קִיַּם , הִתְקַיֵּם . Far more usually these three stems are replaced by three other stems of similar meaning – the Polel, Polal, and the Hithpolel. As can be seen from the stem names, the last consonant is repeated instead of the middle radical being doubled. Fortunately, these stems are similar to the corresponding Piel, Pual, and Hithpael and are easily learned. When there is a preformative in Polel or Polal, it takes a Shewa. The stem vowels are constant throughout and forms are made simply by adding preformatives with Shewa and sufformatives as usual.

A few verbs, like כּוּל instead of using either the Piel, Pual, and Hithpael or the Polel, Polal, and Hithpolel systems of intensive stems use three stems called the Pilpel, Pilpal, and Hithpalpel. Here both consonants are repeated instead of doubling the middle vowel letter. These stems also are easily learned, retaining the stem vowels throughout and adding preformatives and sufformatives just as the Piel, Pual, and Hithpael. There are a few other odd stems such as the Shaphel, etc. for which see Gesenius p 151 f. Typical forms are as follows:

		Polel	Polal	Hithpolel	Pilpel	Pilpal	Hithpalpel
3ms	pf	קֹמֵם	קֹמַם	הִתְקֹמֵם	בִּלְבֵּל	בֻּלְבַּל	הִתְבַּלְבֵּל
2ms	pf	קֹמַמְתָּ	קֹמַמְתָּ	הִתְקֹמַמְתָּ	בִּלְבַּלְתָּ	בֻּלְבַּלְתָּ	הִתְבַּלְבַּלְתָּ
3ms	impf	יְקֹמֵם	יְקֹמַם	יִתְקֹמֵם	יְבַלְבֵּל	יְבֻלְבַּל	יִתְבַּלְבֵּל
2ms	impv	קֹמֵם	--	הִתְקֹמֵם	בַּלְבֵּל	--	הִתְבַּלְבֵּל

Cohortative and Jussive

The cohortative and jussive in Hebrew are only slight modifications of the imperfect tense. Occasionally the imperative gives rise to forms of this kind. The cohortative is the mood of self-encouragement or exhortation. As we should expect, this meaning is reflected in a lengthening of the form as if in pleading. It only applies to the first person sing. and pl. of active stems. To make the cohortative, the ending הָ is added to the form in question. The הָ is treated as a vocal sufforma-

tive causing the vowel just before it to drop to a shewa,
thus: אֶקְטֹל , אֶקְטְלָה , אֶקְטֹל , אֶקְטְלָה . The cohortative He
added to an imperative softens the command to a request.
It is not added to Lamedh-He verbs which already end in
a ה. or ה.. in these forms.

    The jussive is the short, sharp form of semi-
command. It is therefore a somewhat shortened form with
the accent retracted if possible. There are many places
where the jussive and ordinary imperfect will be exactly
alike. In all those forms with an ending either vocalic
or consonantal, the accent can not be retracted and the
forms must remain unchanged. We noticed the same phenomenon in the study of the Waw consecutive with the impf.
(pp. 34 and 39). In fact the jussive in all cases is very
similar to the form of the Waw cons. with the impf. except that it does not have the Waw. The jussive of the
strong verb will only shorten in the Hiphil, thus יַקְטִיל
becomes יַקְטֵל . In the Lamedh-He verb, the jussive is
formed by the apocopation of the final ה.. , thus יִגְלֶה becomes יִגֶל cf. וַיִּגֶל . In the Ayin-Waw verb the jussive
differs again only in Qal and Hiphil, but in the Qal is
slightly different from the corresponding form with Waw
consecutive. Thus יָקוּם becomes יָקֹם (but וַיָּקָם) and
יָקִים becomes יָקֵם (but וַיָּקֶם). The jussive is used only
in the 2nd and 3rd persons sing. and pl. imperfect. The
negative used with the jussive is אַל . "Please do not
kill" would be אַל with the jussive. "Thou shalt not
kill" would be לֹא with the impf. "Kill!" would be
the impv. "Please kill" would be the jussive or the cohortative He on an impv.

Waw Consecutive with the Perfect
    We have already studied (p.25ff) the Waw cons.
with the impf. which has the pointing of the article and
is to be translated as a narrative tense - usually like
a perfect. There is also a Waw consecutive with the pf.
which is usually to be translated like an imperfect. It
is pointed with a vocal shewa just like the ordinary Waw
(Waw conjunctive or copulative), except that sometimes
the accent shifts forward onto the usually toneless endings תָ , תִי , etc. It usually follows an impf. in sequence, thus וְקָטַלְתָ "And thou didst kill," but תִּקְטֹל וְקָבַרְתָ
"Thou wilt kill and thou wilt bury." It may carry on an
imperative: קְטֹל וְקָבַרְתָ "Kill and bury!"
    Beside the two forms, Waw consecutive with the
impf. and with the pf., there are the regular Waw conj.
with the pf., impf., and impv. These, however, seem often to have specialized meanings. וַיִּקְטֹל does not simply

mean "And he will kill." That would normally be expressed
by Waw cons. with the pf. The Waw conj. with the impf.
often seems to have a kind of subjunctive meaning. Thus it
is used with the jussive or the cohortative. Compare also
1 Sam. 4:3 "Let us take unto us from Shiloh the ark of
the covenant of the Lord וְיָבֹא that it may come into our
midst." Also 1 Kings 2:17 "Speak to Solomon the King..
וְיִתֶּן־ that he give to me Abishag." Likewise קוּם וּקְטֹל
does not mean "Rise, Kill!" That would normally be expressed by Waw cons. with the pf.: קוּם וְקָטַלְתָּ . Rather
it means "Rising Kill!" with one verb auxiliary to the
other. Cf. Gen. 42:18 זֹאת עֲשׂוּ וִחְיוּ "This do and live."
The Waw conjunctive with the pf. is not common. It is
relegated by Gesenius to Aramaic influences or doubtful
occurrences. Cf. further Ges. pp. 338f.

Ayin-Yodh Verbs

A few verbs, like בִּין , are like the Ayin-Waw
verbs except that they have a Yodh for the middle radical. Outside of the Qal stem they act exactly like the
Ayin-Waw verbs. In the Qal stem, wherever the Ayin-Waw
verb takes Shureq in the middle, this verb takes Hiriq.
The result is that the impf. Qal looks exactly like the
impf. Hiphil. It even apocopates similarly. Many verbs
appear sometimes as Ayin-Waw and sometimes as Ayin-Yodh.
Typical Qal forms for בִּין are: בִּין,בֹּן , בָּנַתָ , בָּנָה , בֵּן ,
תָּבֶנָּה , תָּבִינִי , וַיָּבֶן , יָבִין .

Vocabulary

שׂוּם , שִׂים	place, put	חֶסֶד	loving kindness, mercy
בִּין	discern (cf. בֵּין between)	שֵׁבֶט	rod, staff, tribe
רוּץ	run	חַיִל	strength, army
לוּן , לִין	lodge, spend the night	עֵת	time (m. but sometimes f.)
חוּל	whirl, writhe, travail	עַתָּה	now
כּוּל	contain, comprehend	תַּחַת	under, instead of
פּוּץ	be scattered	עַד	as noun: perpetuity, age. as conj.: until
יָשַׁע	save, deliver (Joshua-Jesus)	זֶה (m) זֹאת (f)	this (often after noun like att. adj.)
חָזַק	be strong (stat. cf. Hezekiah)	אֵלֶּה (pl. common of above)	these
יָכֹל	be able (impf. יוּכַל)	אַף	also, yea

Exercises

A. Write the key forms of the pf., impf., and impv. of all stems (using Polel intensives) of קוּם and שִׂים .

B. Parse the following forms:

1. חָקֵי 2. יָסֹרוּ 3. מֵשִׂים 4. נְכוֹנוֹתִי 5. תְּרוּמֶינָה 6.תֵּת

7. בִּינִי 8. נְשִׁיכֶם 9. יְהִי 10. וַיָּמָת 11. נְשָׁתוֹ 12.מִקֶם

C. Translate 2 Sam. 7:1-11.

Lesson 18   Verbal Suffixes. Minor Points

Pronoun Suffixes attached to the Verb

There are two ways in which we may write the pronominal object of a verb. The easiest method we have already exemplified (p.55). It consists in using אֵת with the proper suffix, thus: אֹתוֹ . More frequently, however, in Hebrew the pronominal suffix is attached directly to the verb form. The attaching of these suffixes to verbs is more complicated than attaching the genitive pronominal suffixes to nouns because it makes the verbal form somewhat different and harder to recognize. Detailed rules will be found in Gesenius pp.154-164, but general rules for their use will suffice for translation of the Hebrew into English. We shall study the suffixes themselves, then the ways they are connected, then the alterations caused in the verb forms.

The objective suffixes are very similar to the genitive suffixes we have learned, listed on p. 52. A few differences will be noted. The 1 cs. is נִי "me" instead of י. "my." The 3 ms. uses הוּ instead of וֹ more often than is the case with nouns. More confusing are the forms with the so-called energetic Nun. These stronger forms, sometimes used for emphasis but usually to be translated like the normal forms, are made by inserting the syllable נ. the Nun of which usually assimilates yielding the forms as listed in the following table:

Verbal pronominal Suffixes				Suffixes with Energetic Nun			
1 cs	נִי	1 cpl	נוּ	1 cs	נִּי	1 cpl	נוּ
2 ms	ךָ	2 mpl	כֶם	2 ms	ךָּ	(In the pl. only the first person occurs)	
2 fs	ךְ	2 fpl	wanting	2 fs	wanting		
3 ms	הוּ, וֹ	3 mpl	הֶם, ם	3 ms	נּוּ		
3 fs	הָ, הָ 3 fpl		ן	3 fs	נָּה		

The above forms have been given as beginning with a consonant although the Dagesh Forte in the forms with energetic Nun presupposes a full vowel preceding it.

These forms beginning with a consonant will be used when
the verb form ends in a vowel. In those cases where the
verb form ends in a consonant, obviously a helping vowel
must be used. This helping vowel, generally speaking,
will be an A-vowel (either Qames or Pathah) in the pf.
and an E-vowel (usually Sere, occasionally Seghol) in the
impf. and impv. The inf. const. and ptc. of verbs may
take the verbal suffixes as well as the genitive pronominal
suffixes which are used with nouns, but this usage is rare.
The forms in most cases are just like the noun suffixes.

The chief difficulty of recognizing the forms
with objective suffixes and building them, is the change
occasioned in the pointing of the body of the verb by the
addition of the ending. In the first place, the addition
of the suffix causes some of the verbal forms to revert
to a more original stage of the personal sufformatives.
The 3 fs pf. ending הָ‎ now becomes the more original הַ_
The 2 fs pf. ending תְּ‎ now becomes the more original תִי‎
and is indistinguishable from the 1 cs pf. The 2 m pl
pf. תֶּם‎ becomes תוּ‎ . The other sufformatives remain unchanged. This difficulty in using the objective suffixes
is not so great in the impf. and impv. where there are
only three personal sufformatives. These remain unchanged.

In the second place, the addition of the suffixes
causes the tone to shift toward the end of the word. In
consequence of this shift, the vowel of the first syllable
will drop if it can. However, this first vowel is unchangeable in all stems except the Qal, and so there only
it drops to a vocal Shewa. The phenomenon is similar to
that of the normal 2 m and f pl pf. Qal where the Qames
drops to a Shewa before grave endings and the reason is
similar. Also caused by this shift of accent is the pretone lengthening of the original vowel of the second syl-
when the syllable is left open. The Pathah which appears
throughout the pf. before consonantal sufformatives is
dropped to a Shewa before vocalic sufformatives in the
regular verb. But with suffixes in an open syllable before the tone, this Pathah lengthens to a Qames. In the
impf. before suffixes, the Holem of the second radical
usually drops to a vocal Shewa, but before ךָ‎ and כֶם‎ it
drops only to a Qames Hatuph. In the impv. also the vowel
of the second radical has dropped to a Shewa, but the initial vowel is Qames Hatuph. Naturally in the Lamedh-He
verb the false endings הָ‎ and הֶ‎.. are dropped before
adding the suffix. Reference should be made to a paradigm of the verb with suffixes in order to see the above
principles exemplified. These forms are difficult to construct, but our purpose is to recognize, and this is not hard.

Suffixes on the Infinitive Construct

The suffixes used with the inf.const. are usually those used with nouns (cf.p.44). No difficulty should be experienced in identifying these forms in the derived stems as the first part of every such form includes an unchangeable vowel. In the Qal inf.const. the original short vowel, Qames Hatuph, comes back under the first radical to yield forms like קָמְלוֹ . Forms with the energetic Nun are rare with the inf. const. - indeed their main usage is with the impf. anyhow. The suffix on an inf.const. is usually to be translated as the subject of the infinitive. Typical is בְּקָמְלִי "When I killed" or בְּקַמְּלוֹ "When he killed (intensive)."

Doubly Irregular Verbs

There are a few verbs irregular at both the beginning and end, which may cause difficulty. Notable are the Pe-Waw and Lamedh-He verb יָרָה, impf. Hiphil יוֹרֶה, also confusing are נָטָה and נָכָה which are not difficult in unapocopated forms: יִטֶּה and יַכֶּה , but which lose the Dagesh Forte in the apocopated forms making the previous vowel heighten: 3 ms.impf.Qal וַיֵּט but Hiphil: וַיַּט .

The Dual Number

Many Hebrew nouns have a number, in addition to the sing. and pl., which is used to refer to only two of a kind. In Arabic this dual number is much more widely used. In Hebrew it finds its principle use in regard to the members of the body. Feet, hands, etc. are referred to in the dual. The masc. dual ends in ַיִם instead of the pl. ending ִים. Thus, רַגְלַיִם , "two feet."

Vocabulary

זָקֵן	be or become old (stative)	זָקֵן	adj. old; as subst. elder
יָרָה	throw, shoot, instruct (esp. Hiph)	תּוֹרָה	(f) instruction, law
יָדָה	give thanks, praise, (H)	גְּבוּל	boundary, territory
נָטָה	(Cl.I) stretch out, incline	אֲדָמָה	(f) ground, land (cf. אָדָם)
נָכָה	smite (H)	אַמָּה	(f) cubit
לֵבָב	heart, mind (alternative form)	אֶלֶף	one thousand
אַיִל	ram, leader	מְאֹד	abundance;adv.exceedingly

Exercises

A. Write the list on p.47 for קוּם .

B. Translate Gen. 12:1-10 emphasizing verb parsing.

Lesson 19   The Ayin-Ayin Verb

The last important class of irregular verbs to be considered is the Ayin-Ayin or *mediae geminatae* verb. These verbs have the middle radical - in the Ayin position —repeated, such as סָבַב or קָלַל . In several forms they are uncontracted and exactly like the regular verb קָטַל . These forms can easily be recognized and need not concern us. In the contracted forms, one of the repeated letters is lost and the resulting form is very much like that of the Ayin-Waw verb. These verbs are not so common as the Ayin-Waw, but are troublesome to the beginner.

Two basic rules will be helpful in identifying these verbs. (1) The preformative syllable is just like that of the Ayin-Waw verb. That is, it nearly always has a long vowel in an open preformative syllable. (2) Whenever there is an ending of any kind the final consonant is doubled to indicate that one of the two last letters has been lost. There are few exceptions to this helpful rule. In order to preserve this doubling, it follows that all consonantal sufformatives must be added by means of helping vowels - וֹ in the pf. and יֶ in the impf. and impv. Even nouns derived from verbs of this sort may be traced by noting the Dagesh Forte in the second radical when there is an ending. Thus חֹק , חֻקִּים must come from חָקַק. Details of the stems follow:

The Hophal forms without sufformatives are exactly like the same forms of the Ayin-Waw verb. Forms with sufformatives may be easily identified by rule (2) above. E.g.: מוּסָב , תּוּסַבֶּינָה , הוּסַבּוֹת , הוּסַבּוּ , הוּסַב.

The Hiphil also has under the preformative the same vowels as does the Ayin-Waw verb — Sere in pf. and ptc. and Qames everywhere else. The vowel of the monosyllabic stem syllable is an I-vowel, always Sere except that before consonantal sufformatives with their helping vowels it drops to Hiriq, thus: הֵסַב , הֵסַבּוּ , הֲסִבּוֹנוּ, מֵסַב , תְּסִבֶּינָה , יָסַבּוּ , יָסֵב .

The Niphal preformative is again like that of the Ayin-Waw verb - Qames in the pf. and ptc. and everywhere else Hiriq with the first radical doubled. The vowel of the monosyllabic stem syllable is almost always Pathah, thus: נָסָב , תִּפָּבֶינָה , יִּסַּב , נְסַבּוֹתָ , נְסַבָּה , נָסַב.

In the Qal, the ptc., inf. abs., and sometimes the pf. forms do not contract. These forms are self explanatory. In the contracted forms the vowel of the monosyllabic stem syllable is Pathah in the pf. and Holem elsewhere just like the ending of the regular verb קָטַל. With sufformatives, of course, the doubling occurs as explained in rule (2) above. The vowel of the preformative of the impf. is Qames just as in the Ayin-Waw verb. There is an alternative form, however, which is distinctive. In these forms, the preformative with Qames is replaced by the preformative with Hiriq and the next letter doubled in a phenomenon somewhat the reverse of compensatory heightening. Observe that the open syllable with a long vowel is rather equal phonetically to the closed syllable with a short vowel. Apocopated forms are all exactly like those of the Ayin-Waw verb. Cf. the skeleton paradigm.

Just as in the Ayin-Waw verb, the Piel, Pual, and Hithpael are replaced by three stems looking exactly like the Polel, Polal, and Hithpolel of those verbs. In the case of Ayin-Waw verbs, the last consonant was repeated whereas in the Ayin-Ayin verbs it is just that both of the last two consonants are preserved. The names of these stems therefore are slightly different – Po°el, Po'al, and Hithpo'el, where the apostrophe stands for the central Ayin of the type verb פָּעַל , but the resultant forms are exactly like the Polel, Polal, and Hithpolel forms of the Ayin-Waw verb which we have already learned. Some Ayin-Ayin verbs take the Piel הָלַל , and some the Pilpel.

	Qal		Hiphil	Hophal	Niphal	Po'el
pf.3ms	סַב		הֵסֵב	הוּסַב	נָסַב	סוֹבֵב
3fs	סַבָּה		הֵסֵבָּה	הוּסַבָּה	נָסַבָּה	סוֹבֵבָה
2ms	סַבּוֹתָ		הֲסִבּוֹתָ	הוּסַבּוֹתָ	נְסַבּוֹתָ	סוֹבַבְתָּ
inf.con.	סֹב		הָסֵב	הוּסַב	הִסַּב	סוֹבֵב
impf.3ms	יָסֹב יִסֹּב	יִסֹּב	יָסֵב	יוּסַב	יִסַּב	יְסוֹבֵב
2fs	תָּסֹבִּי תִּסֹּבִּי	תִּסֹּבִּי	תָּסֵבִּי	תּוּסַבִּי	תִּסַּבִּי	תְּסוֹבְבִי
2fp	תְּסֻבֶּינָה	תְּסֻבֶּינָה	תְּסִבֶּינָה	תּוּסַבֶּינָה תְּסֻבֶּינָה	תִּסַּבֶּינָה	תְּסוֹבַבְנָה

Metathesis

Metathesis or the transposition of certain letters within a word for euphonic reasons takes place only occasionally in Hebrew. The most frequent instance is the Tau of the prefix of the Hithpael when it appears before sibilants. The Hebrews found it difficult to pronounce the dental before sibilants, so they simply pronounced and wrote the sibilant first. Thus for the Hithpael of שָׁמַר "guard" they wrote הִשְׁתַּמֵּר . Further, after the emphatic sibilant, Sadhe, the s and Tau not only interchange, but also the Tau becomes the emphatic dental, Teth. Thus the Hithpael of צָדַק is הִצְטַדֵּק . Another

occasional change of this Hithpael Tau is, that before a
d or t sound the Tau of the prefix changes to the same
d or t thus doubling it by assimilation. For instance,
the Hithpael of עָמֵא "be unclean," is: הִטַּמֵּא . All these
phenomena are rare except in the case of the important
and irregular verb שָׁחָה "bow down," "worship." This verb
is used only in the Hithpael and metathesis regularly occurs. But it also reduplicates the last letter (original
Waw) like a Hithpolel form. The second Waw gives rise
to endings like the Lamedh-He verb. Important forms are:
הִשְׁתַּחֲוָה , הִשְׁתַּחֲווּ , יִשְׁתַּחֲוֶה , יִשְׁתַּחֲווּ , 3 ms. impf.: וַיִּשְׁתַּחוּ.

Qere and Kethibh

Certain textual critical footnotes in the Hebrew Bible are marked with an asterisk or circle and called
Qere – Kethibh variations. They occur when the written
text contained in the manuscripts before the Masoretic
vocalizers did not agree with their oral tradition or grammatical expectations. Rather than alter the written text
they imposed the correct vowels (as they understood them)
on the disputed word and placed in the margin the consonants which they held to be correct. The Qere (to be read),
therefore consists of the consonants of the margin with
the vowels of the text. The Kethibh (written) consists
of the consonants of the text with vowels to be supplied
by the reader. Some such variations are so frequent and
self-explanatory as not to deserve a footnote and these
are called perpetual Qere, such as הִיא Qere with הוּא
Kethibh in the hybrid form הִוא occurring in the Pentateuch.

Comparison of the Adjective

The comparative degree in Hebrew is most frequently expressed in Hebrew by using מִן in place of our
word "than." Thus, "more righteous than all" is: צַדִּיק מִכֹּל
The superlative is less common, but may be expressed simply by making the adjective definite, sometimes followed
by מִן, בְּ, or a genitive. Thus, 2 Kings 10:3 "the best
of the sons of," is: הַטּוֹב מִבְּנֵי .

Gentilic Ending

Patronymics and tribal names are usually made
by use of the ending ִי. e.g. מוֹאָבִי "Moabite" and מוֹאָבִיָּה
"Moabitess."

The Euphonic Dagesh Forte

In a number of cases the Hebrew text uses a
Dagesh Forte not because of assimilation or grammatical
form, but because of the rhythm of the words. Especially
to be mentioned is the Dagesh Forte Conjunctivum joining

two words the first of which ends in הָ, ָ, or הֶ under certain conditions of accent, and the second begins with an
accented syllable, e.g. הוֹשִׁיעָה נָּא, Hosanna (Ps. 118:25,
note the double n in Matt. 21:15). Cf. further, Ges. p.71ff.

Numerals

The formation and use of the numerals is dis-
cussed at length in Ges. p. 286-292. The subject is a
little involved and the beginner may largely rely on the
use of the vocabulary. The numerals to 10 should be learned. 11 to 19 are written: one ten, two ten, etc. Twenty
is the pl. of ten; thirty the pl. of three; forty the pl.
of four; etc. The strange thing is that the numbers 3 to
10 disagree in gender with the article numbered,the reason not being clear. Ordinal numbers, "second," "third,"
etc. are made by adding the ending י. and inserting another י. , generally, before the last radical. For the
numerals 1-10 see p.85.

Vocabulary

סָבַב	go about, surround	סָבִיב	adv. or prep.: round a-bout
רָבַב	be many, multiply (רָבָה same)	רַב	adj.: much; noun: chief (cf. Rabbi)
הָלַל	praise (P)	רֹב	multitude, abundance
רָעַע	be evil (impf. יֵרַע)	רַע	adj.: bad; noun: evil, distress
חָנַן	show favor	חֵן	grace
חָלַל	pierce; also:pollute (in H also: begin)	אָז	then
שָׁחָה	worship,bow down (Hith)	אֵיכָה or אֵיךְ	how? (interr.) how! (exclam.)
חָדָשׁ	new	פֶּן	lest (used with impf.)
חֹדֶשׁ	new moon, month	יֵשׁ	there is (the opposite of אַיִן) used with suf.
כָּבוֹד	glory, honor (cf. Ichabod & כָּבֵד)	תָּוֶךְ	midst (const. תּוֹךְ . בְּתוֹךְ in the midst of)
זֶרַע	seed, offspring	קֶרֶב	midst; בְּקִרְבִּי within me (cf. קָרַב)
מַטֶּה	rod, staff, tribe	יַעַן	on account of; לְמַעַן in order that, because

Exercises

A. Write the 3 ms impf. of all stems of סָבַב.
B. Translate Gen. 13:1-10.

Lesson 20   Further Notes on Syntax

Agreement of Subject and Predicate

In verbal sentences, the agreement of subject and predicate is not so uniform as in English. Indeed the agreement is often logical rather than grammatical. Thus, a collective noun may be used with either a sing. or pl. verb. Also, if the verb comes first, it often agrees with the first member only of a compound subject. If the subject has already been introduced, the agreement is more usually observed. The 3 ms. or the 3 mp. may either one be used for the impersonal "one says," "they say."

Oaths and Affirmations

The form of oath used frequently in the Old Testament is יְהֹוָה! חַי or חַי נַפְשְׁךָ or similar combinations. After these expressions אִם is used to express an emphatic negative; אִם לֹא is used for an emphatic positive. Both of these particles may be used thus even when the formula of the oath is merely implied.

Conditional Sentences

Sometimes Hebrew expresses a condition without the use of particles by the simple juxtaposition of clauses as: Gen. 44:29 "If you should take also this one ... you would bring down my gray hairs to the grave." More often אִם is used to introduce the protasis; Waw or nothing introduces the apodosis. In general, an impf. in the protasis expresses a condition of eventuality: "If I ascend into heaven" Ps. 139:8; a pf. in the protasis expresses a condition of fact, whether completed or viewed as sure: "If I have found favor in thy sight" Gen. 18:3. The apodasis takes various tenses as the context may demand.

Relative Clauses

Relative clauses may be classed as dependent – those attached to a noun or pronoun, and independent – those which themselves express a substantival idea. The clauses directly dependent on a noun (as: "the man who is sick") may be introduced by אֲשֶׁר but frequently they omit it. They usually include a resumptive pronoun which with the אֲשֶׁר seems tautologous to English ears: "a tree which its seed is in it" Gen. 1:11. This pronoun is, of course, included in the verb of the relative clause if it is the subject of the verb: "The man who killed the horse" הָאִישׁ אֲשֶׁר קָמַל אֶת־הַסּוּס . Independent relative clauses, as "he whom thou lovest is sick" more often omit the sign of relation and also may omit the resumptive pronoun. For examples and further discussion, consult Gesenius p. 485.

APPENDIX Verb Paradigms

	Qal	Piel	Pual	Hiphil	Hophal	Niphal	Hithpael
pf. 1 cs.	כָּתַבְתִּי	כִּתַּבְתִּי	כֻּתַּבְתִּי	הִכְתַּבְתִּי	הָכְתַּבְתִּי	נִכְתַּבְתִּי	הִתְכַּתַּבְתִּי
2 ms.	כָּתַבְתָּ	כִּתַּבְתָּ	כֻּתַּבְתָּ	הִכְתַּבְתָּ	הָכְתַּבְתָּ	נִכְתַּבְתָּ	הִתְכַּתַּבְתָּ
2 fs.	כָּתַבְתְּ	כִּתַּבְתְּ	כֻּתַּבְתְּ	הִכְתַּבְתְּ	הָכְתַּבְתְּ	נִכְתַּבְתְּ	הִתְכַּתַּבְתְּ
3 ms.	כָּתַב	כִּתֵּב	כֻּתַּב	הִכְתִּיב	הָכְתַּב	נִכְתַּב	הִתְכַּתֵּב
3 fs.	כָּתְבָה	כִּתְּבָה	כֻּתְּבָה	הִכְתִּיבָה	הָכְתְּבָה	נִכְתְּבָה	הִתְכַּתְּבָה
1 cp.	כָּתַבְנוּ	כִּתַּבְנוּ	כֻּתַּבְנוּ	הִכְתַּבְנוּ	הָכְתַּבְנוּ	נִכְתַּבְנוּ	הִתְכַּתַּבְנוּ
2 mp.	כְּתַבְתֶּם	כִּתַּבְתֶּם	כֻּתַּבְתֶּם	הִכְתַּבְתֶּם	הָכְתַּבְתֶּם	נִכְתַּבְתֶּם	הִתְכַּתַּבְתֶּם
2 fs.	כְּתַבְתֶּן	כִּתַּבְתֶּן	כֻּתַּבְתֶּן	הִכְתַּבְתֶּן	הָכְתַּבְתֶּן	נִכְתַּבְתֶּן	הִתְכַּתַּבְתֶּן
3 cp.	כָּתְבוּ	כִּתְּבוּ	כֻּתְּבוּ	הִכְתִּיבוּ	הָכְתְּבוּ	נִכְתְּבוּ	הִתְכַּתְּבוּ
inf.ab.	כָּתוֹב	כַּתֵּב	כֻּתֹּב	הַכְתֵּב	הָכְתֵּב	הִכָּתֹב	הִתְכַּתֵּב
cons.	כְּתֹב	כַּתֵּב	כֻּתַּב	הַכְתִּיב	הָכְתֵּב	הִכָּתֵב	הִתְכַּתֵּב
impf. 1 cs.	אֶכְתֹּב	אֲכַתֵּב	אֲכֻתַּב	אַכְתִּיב	אָכְתַּב	אֶכָּתֵב	אֶתְכַּתֵּב
2 ms.	תִּכְתֹּב	תְּכַתֵּב	תְּכֻתַּב	תַּכְתִּיב	תָּכְתַּב	תִּכָּתֵב	תִּתְכַּתֵּב
2 fs.	תִּכְתְּבִי	תְּכַתְּבִי	תְּכֻתְּבִי	תַּכְתִּיבִי	תָּכְתְּבִי	תִּכָּתְבִי	תִּתְכַּתְּבִי
3 ms.	יִכְתֹּב	יְכַתֵּב	יְכֻתַּב	יַכְתִּיב	יָכְתַּב	יִכָּתֵב	יִתְכַּתֵּב
3 fs.	תִּכְתֹּב	תְּכַתֵּב	תְּכֻתַּב	תַּכְתִּיב	תָּכְתַּב	תִּכָּתֵב	תִּתְכַּתֵּב
1 cp.	נִכְתֹּב	נְכַתֵּב	נְכֻתַּב	נַכְתִּיב	נָכְתַּב	נִכָּתֵב	נִתְכַּתֵּב
2 mp.	תִּכְתְּבוּ	תְּכַתְּבוּ	תְּכֻתְּבוּ	תַּכְתִּיבוּ	תָּכְתְּבוּ	תִּכָּתְבוּ	תִּתְכַּתְּבוּ
2 fp.) 3 fp.)	תִּכְתֹּבְנָה	תְּכַתֵּבְנָה	תְּכֻתַּבְנָה	תַּכְתֵּבְנָה	תָּכְתַּבְנָה	תִּכָּתֵבְנָה	תִּתְכַּתֵּבְנָה
3 mp.	יִכְתְּבוּ	יְכַתְּבוּ	יְכֻתְּבוּ	יַכְתִּיבוּ	יָכְתְּבוּ	יִכָּתְבוּ	יִתְכַּתְּבוּ
cons.	וַיִּכְתֹּב	וַיְכַתֵּב	וַיְכֻתַּב	וַיַּכְתֵּב	וַיָּכְתַּב	וַיִּכָּתֵב	וַיִּתְכַּתֵּב
impv. 2 ms.	כְּתֹב	כַּתֵּב		הַכְתֵּב		הִכָּתֵב	הִתְכַּתֵּב
2 fs.	כִּתְבִי	כַּתְּבִי		הַכְתִּיבִי		הִכָּתְבִי	הִתְכַּתְּבִי
2 mp.	כִּתְבוּ	כַּתְּבוּ		הַכְתִּיבוּ		הִכָּתְבוּ	הִתְכַּתְּבוּ
2 fp.	כְּתֹבְנָה	כַּתֵּבְנָה		הַכְתֵּבְנָה		הִכָּתֵבְנָה	הִתְכַּתֵּבְנָה
act. ptc.	כֹּתֵב	מְכַתֵּב	מְכֻתָּב	מַכְתִּיב			מִתְכַּתֵּב
pass.	כָּתוּב			מְכֻתָּב		מָכְתָּב	נִכְתָּב

pf.	Qal	Piel	Pual	Hiphil	Hophal	Niphal	Hithpael
1 cs.	בָּנִיתִי	בִּנִּיתִי	בֻּנֵּיתִי	הִבְנֵיתִי	הָבְנֵיתִי	נִבְנֵיתִי	הִתְבַּנֵּיתִי
2 ms.	בָּנִיתָ	בִּנִּיתָ	בֻּנֵּיתָ	הִבְנֵיתָ	הָבְנֵיתָ	נִבְנֵיתָ	הִתְבַּנֵּיתָ
2 fs.	בָּנִית	בִּנִּית	בֻּנֵּית	הִבְנֵית	הָבְנֵית	נִבְנֵית	הִתְבַּנֵּית
3 ms.	בָּנָה	בִּנָּה	בֻּנָּה	הִבְנָה	הָבְנָה	נִבְנָה	הִתְבַּנָּה
3 fs.	בָּנְתָה	בִּנְּתָה	בֻּנְּתָה	הִבְנְתָה	הָבְנְתָה	נִבְנְתָה	הִתְבַּנְּתָה
1 cp.	בָּנִינוּ	בִּנִּינוּ	בֻּנֵּינוּ	הִבְנֵינוּ	הָבְנֵינוּ	נִבְנֵינוּ	הִתְבַּנֵּינוּ
2 mp.	בְּנִיתֶם	בִּנִּיתֶם	בֻּנֵּיתֶם	הִבְנֵיתֶם	הָבְנֵיתֶם	נִבְנֵיתֶם	הִתְבַּנֵּיתֶם
2 fp.	בְּנִיתֶן	בִּנִּיתֶן	בֻּנֵּיתֶן	הִבְנֵיתֶן	הָבְנֵיתֶן	נִבְנֵיתֶן	הִתְבַּנֵּיתֶן
3 cp.	בָּנוּ	בִּנּוּ	בֻּנּוּ	הִבְנוּ	הָבְנוּ	נִבְנוּ	הִתְבַּנּוּ
inf.ab.	בָּנֹה	בַּנֹּה	בֻּנֹּה	הַבְנֵה	הָבְנֵה	הִבָּנֹה	הִתְבַּנֹּה
const.	בְּנוֹת	בַּנּוֹת	בֻּנּוֹת	הַבְנוֹת	הָבְנוֹת	הִבָּנוֹת	הִתְבַּנּוֹת
impf. 1 cs.	אֶבְנֶה	אֲבַנֶּה	אֲבֻנֶּה	אַבְנֶה	אָבְנֶה	אֶבָּנֶה	אֶתְבַּנֶּה
2 ms.	תִּבְנֶה	תְּבַנֶּה	תְּבֻנֶּה	תַּבְנֶה	תָּבְנֶה	תִּבָּנֶה	תִּתְבַּנֶּה
2 fs.	תִּבְנִי	תְּבַנִּי	תְּבֻנִּי	תַּבְנִי	תָּבְנִי	תִּבָּנִי	תִּתְבַּנִּי
3 ms.	יִבְנֶה	יְבַנֶּה	יְבֻנֶּה	יַבְנֶה	יָבְנֶה	יִבָּנֶה	יִתְבַּנֶּה
3 fs.	תִּבְנֶה	תְּבַנֶּה	תְּבֻנֶּה	תַּבְנֶה	תָּבְנֶה	תִּבָּנֶה	תִּתְבַּנֶּה
1 cp.	נִבְנֶה	נְבַנֶּה	נְבֻנֶּה	נַבְנֶה	נָבְנֶה	נִבָּנֶה	נִתְבַּנֶּה
2 mp.	תִּבְנוּ	תְּבַנּוּ	תְּבֻנּוּ	תַּבְנוּ	תָּבְנוּ	תִּבָּנוּ	תִּתְבַּנּוּ
2 fp. 3 fp. (·)	תִּבְנֶינָה	תְּבַנֶּינָה	תְּבֻנֶּינָה	תַּבְנֶינָה	תָּבְנֶינָה	תִּבָּנֶינָה	תִּתְבַּנֶּינָה
3 mp.	יִבְנוּ	יְבַנּוּ	יְבֻנּוּ	יַבְנוּ	יָבְנוּ	יִבָּנוּ	יִתְבַּנּוּ
۱cons.	וַיִּבֶן	וַיְבַן	וַיְבֻן	וַיֶּבֶן	וַיָּבֶן	וַיִּבֶן	וַיִּתְבַּן
impv. 2 ms.	בְּנֵה	בַּנֵּה		הַבְנֵה		הִבָּנֵה	הִתְבַּנֵּה
2 fs.	בְּנִי	בַּנִּי		הַבְנִי		הִבָּנִי	הִתְבַּנִּי
2 mp.	בְּנוּ	בַּנּוּ		הַבְנוּ		הִבָּנוּ	הִתְבַּנּוּ
2 fp.	בְּנֶינָה	בַּנֶּינָה		הַבְנֶינָה		הִבָּנֶינָה	הִתְבַּנֶּינָה
act. ptc.	בֹּנֶה	מְבַנֶּה	מְבֻנֶּה	מַבְנֶה			מִתְבַּנֶּה
pass.	בָּנוּי		מְבֻנֶּה		מָבְנֶה	נִבְנֶה	

pf.	Qal	(Piel, Pual, and Hithpael are the same as קְטֵל)		Hiphil	Hophal	Niphal
1 cs.	נָפַלְתִּי			הִפַּלְתִּי	הֻפַּלְתִּי	נִפַּלְתִּי
2 ms.	נָפַלְתָּ	as קְטַל		הִפַּלְתָּ	הֻפַּלְתָּ	נִפַּלְתָּ
2 fs.	נָפַלְתְּ	— — —		הִפַּלְתְּ	הֻפַּלְתְּ	נִפַּלְתְּ
3 ms.	נָפַל			הִפִּיל	הֻפַּל	נִפַּל
3 fs.	נָפְלָה			הִפִּילָה	הֻפְּלָה	נִפְּלָה
1 cp.	נָפַלְנוּ			הִפַּלְנוּ	הֻפַּלְנוּ	נִפַּלְנוּ
2 mp.	נְפַלְתֶּם			הִפַּלְתֶּם	הֻפַּלְתֶּם	נִפַּלְתֶּם
2 fp.	נְפַלְתֶּן			הִפַּלְתֶּן	הֻפַּלְתֶּן	נִפַּלְתֶּן
3 cp.	נָפְלוּ			הִפִּילוּ	הֻפְּלוּ	נִפְּלוּ
		Pathah stat.	Sere stat.			
inf. abs.	נָפוֹל			הַפֵּל	הֻפֵּל	הִנָּפֹל
const.	נְפֹל	גֶּשֶׁת	תֵּת	הַפִּיל	הֻפַּל	הִנָּפֵל
impf. 1 cs.	אֶפֹּל	אֶגַּשׁ	אֶתֵּן	אַפִּיל	אֻפַּל	אֶנָּפֵל
2 ms.	תִּפֹּל	תִּגַּשׁ	תִּתֵּן	תַּפִּיל	תֻּפַּל	תִּנָּפֵל
2 fs.	תִּפְּלִי	תִּגְּשִׁי	תִּתְּנִי	תַּפִּילִי	תֻּפְּלִי	תִּנָּפְלִי
3 ms.	יִפֹּל	יִגַּשׁ	יִתֵּן	יַפִּיל	יֻפַּל	יִנָּפֵל
3 fs.	תִּפֹּל	תִּגַּשׁ	תִּתֵּן	תַּפִּיל	תֻּפַּל	תִּנָּפֵל
1 cp.	נִפֹּל	נִגַּשׁ	נִתֵּן	נַפִּיל	נֻפַּל	נִנָּפֵל
2 mp.	תִּפְּלוּ	תִּגְּשׁוּ	תִּתְּנוּ	תַּפִּילוּ	תֻּפְּלוּ	תִּנָּפְלוּ
2 & 3 fp.	תִּפֹּלְנָה	תִּגַּשְׁנָה	תִּתֵּנָּה	תַּפֵּלְנָה	תֻּפַּלְנָה	תִּנָּפַלְנָה
3 mp.	יִפְּלוּ	יִגְּשׁוּ	יִתְּנוּ	יַפִּילוּ	יֻפְּלוּ	יִנָּפְלוּ
ו cons.	וַיִּפֹּל	וַיִּגַּשׁ	וַיִּתֵּן	וַיַּפֵּל	וַיֻּפַּל	וַיִּנָּפֵל
impv. 2 ms.	נְפֹל	גַּשׁ	תֵּן	הַפֵּל		הִנָּפֵל
2 fs.	נִפְלִי	גְּשִׁי	תְּנִי	הַפִּילִי		הִנָּפְלִי
2 mp.	נִפְלוּ	גְּשׁוּ	תְּנוּ	הַפִּילוּ		הֵנָּפְלוּ
2 fp.	נְפֹלְנָה	גַּשְׁנָה	תֵּנָּה	הַפֵּלְנָה		הִנָּפַלְנָה
act.ptc.	נֹפֵל	נֹגֵשׁ	נֹתֵן	מַפִּיל		
pass.	נָפוּל	נָגוּשׁ	נָתוּן		מֻפָּל	נִפָּל

pf.	Qal	Piel, Pual, and Hithpael Pe-Waw verbs like קָטַל	Hiphil	Hophal	Niphal	Pe-Yodh Hiphil
1 cs.	יָרַשְׁתִּי		הוֹרַשְׁתִּי	הוּרַשְׁתִּי	נוֹרַשְׁתִּי	הֵיטַבְתִּי
2 ms.	יָרַשְׁתָּ		הוֹרַשְׁתָּ	הוּרַשְׁתָּ	נוֹרַשְׁתָּ	הֵיטַבְתָּ
2 fs.	יָרַשְׁתְּ		הוֹרַשְׁתְּ	הוּרַשְׁתְּ	נוֹרַשְׁתְּ	הֵיטַבְתְּ
3 ms.	יָרַשׁ		הוֹרִישׁ	הוּרַשׁ	נוֹרַשׁ	הֵיטִיב
3 fs.	יָרְשָׁה	— — — —	הוֹרִישָׁה	הוּרְשָׁה	נוֹרְשָׁה	הֵיטִיבָה
1 cp.	יָרַשְׁנוּ		הוֹרַשְׁנוּ	הוּרַשְׁנוּ	נוֹרַשְׁנוּ	הֵיטַבְנוּ
2 mp.	יְרַשְׁתֶּם		הוֹרַשְׁתֶּם	הוּרַשְׁתֶּם	נוֹרַשְׁתֶּם	הֵיטַבְתֶּם
2 fp.	יְרַשְׁתֶּן		הוֹרַשְׁתֶּן	הוּרַשְׁתֶּן	נוֹרַשְׁתֶּן	הֵיטַבְתֶּן
3 cp.	יָרְשׁוּ		הוֹרִישׁוּ	הוּרְשׁוּ	נוֹרְשׁוּ	הֵיטִיבוּ
inf. ab.	יָרוֹשׁ Sere stat.		הוֹרֵשׁ	הוּרֵשׁ	הִנָּרֹשׁ	הֵיטֵב
const.	רֶשֶׁת שֶׁבֶת		הוֹרִישׁ	הוּרֵשׁ	הִנָּרֹשׁ	הֵיטִיב
impf.						
1 cs.	אִירַשׁ אֵשֵׁב		אוֹרִישׁ	אוּרַשׁ	אִנָּרֵשׁ	אֵיטִיב
2 ms.	תִּירַשׁ תֵּשֵׁב		תּוֹרִישׁ	תּוּרַשׁ	תִּנָּרֵשׁ	תֵּיטִיב
2 fs.	תִּירְשִׁי תֵּשְׁבִי		תּוֹרִישִׁי	תּוּרְשִׁי	תִּנָּרְשִׁי	תֵּיטִיבִי
3 ms.	יִירַשׁ יֵשֵׁב		יוֹרִישׁ	יוּרַשׁ	יִנָּרֵשׁ	יֵיטִיב
3 fs.	תִּירַשׁ תֵּשֵׁב		תּוֹרִישׁ	תּוּרַשׁ	תִּנָּרֵשׁ	תֵּיטִיב
1 cp.	נִירַשׁ נֵשֵׁב		נוֹרִישׁ	נוּרַשׁ	נִנָּרֵשׁ	נֵיטִיב
2 mp.	תִּירְשׁוּ תֵּשְׁבוּ		תּוֹרִישׁוּ	תּוּרְשׁוּ	תִּנָּרְשׁוּ	תֵּיטִיבוּ
2 & 3 fp.	תִּירַשְׁנָה תֵּשַׁבְנָה		תּוֹרֵשְׁנָה	תּוּרַשְׁנָה	תִּנָּרַשְׁנָה	תֵּיטַבְנָה
3 mp.	יִירְשׁוּ יֵשְׁבוּ		יוֹרִישׁוּ	יוּרְשׁוּ	יִנָּרְשׁוּ	יֵיטִיבוּ
ו cons.	וַיִּירַשׁ וַיֵּשֶׁב		וַיּוֹרֶשׁ	וַיּוּרַשׁ	וַיִּוָּרֶשׁ	וַיֵּיטֶב
impv.						
2 ms.	רַשׁ שֵׁב		הוֹרֵשׁ		הִוָּרֵשׁ	הֵיטֵב
2 fs.	רְשִׁי שְׁבִי		הוֹרִישִׁי		הִוָּרְשִׁי	הֵיטִיבִי
2 mp.	רְשׁוּ שְׁבוּ		הוֹרִישׁוּ		הִוָּרְשׁוּ	הֵיטִיבוּ
2 fp.	רַשְׁנָה שֵׁבְנָה		הוֹרֵשְׁנָה		הִוָּרַשְׁנָה	הֵיטֵבְנָה
act. ptc.	יֹרֵשׁ יֹשֵׁב		מוֹרִישׁ			מֵיטִיב
pass.	יָרוּשׁ יָשׁוּב			מוּרָשׁ	נוֹרָשׁ	

	Qal	Polel	Polal	Hiphil	Hophal	Niphal	Hithpolel
pf. 1 cs.	קַמְתִּי	קֹמַמְתִּי	קֹמַמְתִּי	הֲקִמֹתִי	הוּקַמְתִּי	נְקוּמֹתִי	הִתְקֹמַמְתִּי
2 ms.	קַמְתָּ	קֹמַמְתָּ	קֹמַמְתָּ	הֲקִימֹתָ	הוּקַמְתָּ	נְקוּמֹתָ	הִתְקֹמַמְתָּ
2 fs.	קַמְתְּ	קֹמַמְתְּ	קֹמַמְתְּ	הֲקִימֹת	הוּקַמְתְּ	נְקוּמֹת	הִתְקֹמַמְתְּ
3 ms.	קָם	קֹמֵם	קֹמַם	הֵקִים	הוּקַם	נָקוֹם	הִתְקֹמֵם
3 fs.	קָמָה	קֹמֲמָה	קֹמֲמָה	הֵקִימָה	הוּקְמָה	נָקוֹמָה	הִתְקֹמֲמָה
1 cp.	קַמְנוּ	קֹמַמְנוּ	קֹמַמְנוּ	הֲקִימֹנוּ	הוּקַמְנוּ	נְקוּמֹנוּ	הִתְקֹמַמְנוּ
2 mp.	קַמְתֶּם	קֹמַמְתֶּם	קֹמַמְתֶּם	הֲקִימֹתֶם	הוּקַמְתֶּם	נְקוּמֹתֶם	הִתְקֹמַמְתֶּם
2 fp.	קַמְתֶּן	קֹמַמְתֶּן	קֹמַמְתֶּן	הֲקִימֹתֶן	הוּקַמְתֶּן	נְקֻמֹתֶן	הִתְקֹמַמְתֶּן
3 cp.	קָמוּ	קֹמֲמוּ	קֹמֲמוּ	הֵקִימוּ	הוּקְמוּ	נָקוֹמוּ	הִתְקֹמֲמוּ
inf.ab.	קוֹם			הָקֵם		נָקוֹם or הִקּוֹם	
const.	קוּם	קֹמֵם	קֹמַם	הָקִים	הוּקַם	הִקּוֹם	הִתְקֹמֵם
impf. 1 cs.	אָקוּם	אֲקֹמֵם	אֲקֹמַם	אָקִים	אוּקַם	אֶקּוֹם	אֶתְקֹמֵם
2 ms.	תָּקוּם	תְּקֹמֵם	תְּקֹמַם	תָּקִים	תּוּקַם	תִּקּוֹם	תִּתְקֹמֵם
2 fs.	תָּקוּמִי	תְּקֹמֲמִי	תְּקֹמֲמִי	תָּקִימִי	תּוּקְמִי	תִּקּוֹמִי	תִּתְקֹמֲמִי
3 ms.	יָקוּם	יְקֹמֵם	יְקֹמַם	יָקִים	יוּקַם	יִקּוֹם	יִתְקֹמֵם
3 fs.	תָּקוּם	תְּקֹמֵם	תְּקֹמַם	תָּקִים	תּוּקַם	תִּקּוֹם	תִּתְקֹמֵם
1 cp.	נָקוּם	נְקֹמֵם	נְקֹמַם	נָקִים	נוּקַם	נִקּוֹם	נִתְקֹמֵם
2 mp.	תָּקוּמוּ	תְּקֹמֲמוּ	תְּקֹמֲמוּ	תָּקִימוּ	תּוּקְמוּ	תִּקּוֹמוּ	תִּתְקֹמֲמוּ
2 & 3 fp	תְּקוּמֶינָה תָּקֹמְנָה	תְּקֹמֵמְנָה	תְּקֹמַמְנָה	תְּקִימֶינָה*תָּקֵמְנָה	תּוּקַמְנָה	תִּקּוֹמְנָה	תִּתְקֹמַמְנָה
3 mp.	יָקוּמוּ	יְקֹמֲמוּ	יְקֹמֲמוּ	יָקִימוּ	יוּקְמוּ	יִקּוֹמוּ	יִתְקֹמֲמוּ
ו **cons.**	וַיָּקָם וַיָּקֶם	וַיְקֹמֵם	וַיְקֹמַם	וַיָּקֶם	וַיּוּקַם	וַיִּקּוֹם	וַיִּתְקֹמֵם
impv. 2 ms.	קוּם	קֹמֵם		הָקֵם		הִקּוֹם	הִתְקֹמֵם
2 fs.	קוּמִי	קֹמֲמִי		הָקִימִי		הִקּוֹמִי	הִתְקֹמֲמִי
2 mp.	קוּמוּ	קֹמֲמוּ		הָקִימוּ		הִקּוֹמוּ	הִתְקֹמֲמוּ
2 fp.	קֹמְנָה	קֹמֵמְנָה		הָקֵמְנָה		הִקּוֹמְנָה	הִתְקֹמַמְנָה
ptc. a.	קָם	מְקֹמֵם		מֵקִים			מִתְקֹמֵם
p.	קוּם		מְקֹמָם		מוּקָם	נָקוֹם	

*(or תְּקוּמֶינָה)   *(or תְּקִימֶינָה)
(Holem of intensives not usually defective)

pf.	Qal	Intensives	Hiphil	Hophal	Niphal
1 cs.	סַבּוֹתִי	like קַמֵּל or Ayin-Waw verb	הֲסִבּוֹתִי	הוּסַבּוֹתִי	נְסַבּוֹתִי
2 ms.	סַבּוֹתָ		הֲסִבּוֹתָ	הוּסַבּוֹתָ	נְסַבּוֹתָ
2 fs.	סַבּוֹת		הֲסִבּוֹת	הוּסַבּוֹת	נְסַבּוֹת
3 ms.	סַב		הֵסֵב	הוּסַב	נָסַב
3 fs.	סַבָּה		הֵסֵבָּה	הוּסַבָּה	נָסַבָּה
1 cp.	סַבּוֹנוּ		הֲסִבּוֹנוּ	הוּסַבּוֹנוּ	נְסַבּוֹנוּ
2 mp.	סַבּוֹתֶם		הֲסִבּוֹתֶם	הוּסַבּוֹתֶם	נְסַבּוֹתֶם
2 fp.	סַבּוֹתֶן		הֲסִבּוֹתֶן	הוּסַבּוֹתֶן	נְסַבּוֹתֶן
3 cp.	סַבּוּ		הֵסֵבּוּ	הוּסַבּוּ	נָסַבּוּ
inf.abs.	סָבוֹב		הָסֵב		הִסֵּב
const.	סֹב	Alternative Qal form	הָסֵב		הִסֵּב
impf. 1 cs.	אָסֹב	אֶסֹּב	אָסֵב	אוּסַב	אֶסַּב
2 ms.	תָּסֹב	תִּסֹּב	תָּסֵב	תּוּסַב	תִּסַּב
2 fs.	תָּסֹבִּי	תִּסֹּבִּי	תָּסֵבִּי	תּוּסַבִּי	תִּסַּבִּי
3 ms.	יָסֹב	יִסֹּב	יָסֵב	יוּסַב	יִסַּב
3 fs.	תָּסֹב	תִּסֹּב	תָּסֵב	תּוּסַב	תִּסַּב
1 cp.	נָסֹב	נִסֹּב	נָסֵב	נוּסַב	נִסַּב
2 mp.	תָּסֹבּוּ	תִּסֹּבּוּ	תָּסֵבּוּ	תּוּסַבּוּ	תִּסַּבּוּ
2 & 3 fp.	תְּסֻבֶּינָה	תִּסֹּבְנָה	תָּסִבֶּינָה	תּוּסַבֶּינָה	תִּסַּבֶּינָה
3 mp.	יָסֹבּוּ	יִסֹּבּוּ	יָסֵבּוּ	יוּסַבּוּ	יִסַּבּוּ
impv. 2 ms.	סֹב		הָסֵב		הִסַּב
2 fs.	סֹבִּי		הָסֵבִּי		הִסַּבִּי
2 mp.	סֹבּוּ		הָסֵבּוּ		הִסַּבּוּ
2 fp.	סֻבֶּינָה		הֲסִבֶּינָה		הִסַּבֶּינָה
act.ptc.	סֹבֵב		מֵסֵב		
pass.	סָבוּב			מוּסָב	נָסָב

(Impf. with ו cons. like Ayin-Waw verb)

Hebrew – English Vocabulary

(The selection of words in the Grammar has been made in accordance with the frequency lists of W.R.Harper (which are not always accurate) supplemented with other material. The more common words are used in the exercises. A few additional words are added in this vocabulary and marked with an asterisk. This list includes all the verbs used more than 100 times in the Old Testament, all the nouns used more than 200 times, most of the important particles, and a few additional words of interest. All should be learned. The numbers after certain words refer to pages where more information is given on them.)

א

אָב   father

אָבַד*   perish

אֶבֶן   stone (f)

אָדוֹן*   lord, אֲדֹנָי 'Lord

אָדָם   mankind, man

אֲדָמָה   ground, land(f)

אָהֵב*   love

אֹהֶל   tent

אָז   then

אָח   brother (14)

אַחַר   after (56)

אֵיךְ or אֵיכָה   how?how! (73)

אַיִל   ram, leader

אִישׁ   man

אָכַל   eat(Q)consume(P)

אֶל   unto, into, towards (56)

אֵל*   God

אֵלֶּה   these(see זֶה, 66)

אֱלֹהִים   God (14)

אֶלֶף   thousand

אִם   if (59)

אֵם   mother (f)

אַמָּה   cubit (f)

אָמַן*   believe(H)confirm(N)

אָמַר   say (31)

ב

אָסַף   gather

אַף   also, yea

אַף*   nose, anger

אַרְבַּע*   four

אָרוֹן*   chest, ark

אֶרֶץ   earth, land (17)

אִשָּׁה   woman, wife (f, 14)

אֲשֶׁר   who,which,he who (56)

אֵת   sign of accus.(55)

אֵת   with (59)

בְּ   in, by means of

בֶּגֶד   garment

בְּהֵמָה   cattle (f)

בּוֹא   enter, go in (63)

בּוֹשׁ   be ashamed (63)

בָּטַח*   trust

בִּין   discern

בֵּין   between

בַּיִת   house

בָּכָה*   weep

בֵּן   son

בָּנָה   build

בֹּקֶר*   morning

בָּקַשׁ   seek, search (P)

בָּרָא   create (17)

בְּרִית covenant (f, 14)

בָּרַךְ kneel(Q),bless(P)

בָּשָׂר* flesh

בַּת daughter

ג

גָּאַל* redeem

גְּבוּל boundary,territory

גָּדוֹל great

גָּדַל* be great

גּוֹי nation (63)

גּוּר sojourn

גָּלָה* uncover, remove

ד

דָּבַק cleave to (43)

דָּבָר word

דִּבֶּר speak (P)

דָּם blood

דֶּרֶךְ way, road

דָּרַשׁ seek, inquire of

ה

הָיָה be,become,come to pass

הָלַךְ go(Q)march(P)lead(H)

הָלַל praise (P)

הִנֵּה or הֵן behold! (63)

הַר mountain

הָרַג kill,slay

ו

וַיֹּאמֶר and he said (28)

וַיְהִי and it came to pass (56)

וַיֵּלֶךְ and he went (43)

ז

זֹאת this (f, see זֶה)

זָבַח sacrifice (31)

זֶבַח a sacrifice

זֶה this (66)

זָהָב gold

זָכַר remember

זָקֵן be old (73)

זָקֵן old, an elder (69)

זֶרַע seed, offspring

ח

חָדָשׁ new

חֹדֶשׁ new moon, month

חוּל whirl,writhe,travail

חָזַק be strong

חָטָא sin(Q)purify (P)

חַטָּאת* sin,sin offering (f)

חַי* living, life

חָיָה live(Q)save alive(P,H)

חַיִל strength, army

חָלַל pierce,pollute(Q)begin(H)

חָמֵשׁ* five

חָנָה* encamp

חָנַן show favor

חֵן grace

חֶסֶד loving kindness,mercy

חֶרֶב sword (f)

חָשַׁב* reckon, impute

ט

טוֹב good

טָמֵא* be unclean

י

יָד* hand (f)

יָדָה* give thanks (H)

יָדַע know (Q)make known(H)

יְהוָה LORD (7)

יוֹם day

יָטַב be good(Q)do good(H, 51)

יָכֹל be able (66)

יָלַד bear a child (51)

יָם sea (31)

יָסַף add(Q & H, 51)

יַעַן	on account of (73)	לָחַם	fight (N)
יָצָא	go out (51)	לֶחֶם	bread, food
יָרֵא	fear, reverence (51)	לָכַד	take, capture
יָרַד	go down (51)	לַיְלָה	night (63)
יָרָה	throw, instruct (esp. H)	לָמַד	learn (Q) teach (P)
יָרַשׁ	possess (Q) disposses (H)	לְמַעַן	in order that, because (73)
יֵשׁ	there is (73)	לָקַח	take (47)
יָשַׁב	sit, dwell (51)		

מ

יָשַׁע	save, deliver	מְאֹד	abundance, exceedingly (69)
יָתַר*	be left over	מֵאָה*	hundred (f)

כ

		מַדּוּעַ	wherefore? why?
כְּ	as, like	מָה, מַה־, or מֶה	what? (47)
כָּבֵד	be heavy, rich (Q) honor (P)	מוֹעֵד*	appointed time, meeting
כָּבוֹד	glory, honor (73)	מוּת	die (Q) kill (H)
כֹּהֵן	priest	מָוֶת	death
כּוּל	contain, comprehend	מִזְבֵּחַ	altar (36)
כּוּן	establish (H) be estab. (N)	מַחֲנֶה*	encampment
כִּי	that, because, if (43)	מַטֶּה	rod, staff, tribe
כָּל־ or כֹּל	all, every	מִי	who?
כָּלָה	be complete, (Q) finish (P)	מַיִם*	waters, water
כְּלִי*	utensil, vessel	מָלֵא*	be full (Q) fill (P)
כֵּן	so, thus (59)	מַלְאָךְ*	messenger, angel
כָּסָה*	cover (P)	מִלְחָמָה	war, battle (f)
כֶּסֶף	silver, money	מָלַךְ	reign
כַּף	palm of hand, sole of foot	מֶלֶךְ	king
כָּפַר	make atonement (P)	מִן	from (56)
כָּרַת	cut, cut off (14)	מַעֲשֶׂה	deed, work (40)
כָּשַׁל	stumble	מִצְוָה	commandment (f)
כָּתַב	write	מָקוֹם	place
		מָשַׁל	rule

ל

		מִשְׁפָּחָה*	family, clan (f)
לְ	to, for	מִשְׁפָּט	judgment

נ

לֹא	not (17)		
לֵב	heart, mind		
לֵבָב	heart, mind	נָא	I pray, please (63)
לָבַשׁ	put on (clothes, etc.)	נָבִיא	prophet
לוּן or לִין	lodge	נָגַד	declare (H)

נָגַע	touch,strike(Q)reach(H)	עַם	people
נֶגַע	stroke, plague	עִם	with,along with
נָגַשׁ	approach (47)	עִמָּד-	with (63,a form of עִם)
נַחֲלָה*	property,inheritance(f)	עָמַד	stand (23)
נָטָה	stretch out,incline (69)	עָנָה	answer(Q) afflict (P)
נָכָה	smite (H)	עֵץ	tree,wood
נָסַע*	journey	עָשָׂה	do, make
נַעַר	boy, servant	עֶשֶׂר*	ten
נַעֲרָה	girl (f)	עֵת	time
נָפַל	fall (47)	עַתָּה	now
נֶפֶשׁ	soul,person,life(f)	**פ**	
נָצַל	snatch,deliver(H)	פֶּן	lest (73)
נָשָׂא	lift up (47)	פָּנָה*	turn
נָתַן	give,put,set (47)	פָּנִים	face,faces (28)
ס		פָּקַד	visit
סָבַב	go about,surround	פּוּץ	be scattered
סָבִיב	round about (73)	פֶּה	mouth (56)
סוּס	horse	**צ**	
סוּר	turn aside	צֹאן	sheep,flock (f)
סָפַר	count	צִוָּה	command (P)
סֵפֶר	book	**ק**	
ע		קָבַר	bury
עָבַד	serve	קָדַשׁ	be holy(Q)sanctify(P,H,43)
עֶבֶד	servant	קֹדֶשׁ	holiness
עָבַר	cross over,transgress	קָדֹשׁ	holy
עַד	age, until (66)	קוֹל	voice,sound
עָוֹן*	iniquity	קוּם	rise, stand
עֹלָה	burnt offering (f)	קָרָא	call,proclaim; also:meet
עוֹלָם	age,eon,eternity	קָרַב	draw near(Q)offer(H) (31)
עָזַב*	forsake	קֶרֶב	midst
עַיִן	fountain,eye (20)	קָרָה or קָרָא	befall,meet
עִיר*	city (f)	**ר**	
עַל	on,beside,concerning (56)	רָאָה	see (43)
עַל-כֵּן	therefore (59)	רֹאשׁ*	head
עָלָה	go up	רֹב	multitude,abundance
עֶלְיוֹן*	high,Most High	רַב	much, chief (73)

רָבַב	be many, multiply
רָבָה	(same as רָבַב)
רֶגֶל*	foot (f)
רָדַף	pursue
רוּחַ	breath, wind, spirit
רוּם	be high
רוּץ	run
רָכַב	ride (43)
רֵעַ*	friend
רָעָה*	pasture, feed
רָעַע	be evil (73)
רַע	bad, distress (73)
רַק	only, surely
רָשָׁע	wicked (40)

ש

שָׂדֶה	field (56)
שׂוֹם or שִׂים	place, put
שָׂנֵא	hate
שַׂר	prince
שָׂרַף	burn

שׁ

שָׁאַל*	ask
שָׁאַר*	remain, be left over
שֵׁבֶט	rod, staff, tribe
שָׁבַע*	swear
שֶׁבַע*	seven
שָׁבַר	break in pieces
שָׁבַת	cease, rest
שׁוּב	turn back, return
שָׁחָה	worship, bow down (72, 73)
שָׁחַת	go to ruin (Q) destroy (P)
שָׁכַב*	lie down
שָׁכַם	rise early (H)
שָׁכַן	dwell
שָׁלוֹם	peace, welfare
שָׁלוֹשׁ*	three

שָׁלַח	send (Q) send away (P, 28)
שָׁלַךְ	throw, cast (H)
שָׁלֵם*	be complete (Q) recompense (P)
שָׁם	there, שָׁמָּה thither
שֵׁם	name
שָׁמַד	be destroyed (N)
שָׁמַיִם	heavens, sky
שְׁמֹנֶה*	eight
שָׁמַע	hear
שָׁמַר	guard
שָׁנָה	year
שְׁנַיִם*	two (f. שְׁתַּיִם)
שַׁעַר*	gate
שָׁפַט	judge
שֵׁשׁ*	six
שָׁתָה	drink

ת

תָּוֶךְ	midst (73)
תּוֹרָה	instruction, law
תַּחַת	under, instead of
תָּם	integrity (63)
תִּשַׁע*	nine

The Numerals to Ten

	m	f
one	אֶחָד	אַחַת
two	שְׁנַיִם	שְׁתַּיִם
three	שָׁלוֹשׁ	שְׁלֹשָׁה
four	אַרְבַּע	אַרְבָּעָה
five	חָמֵשׁ	חֲמִשָּׁה
six	שֵׁשׁ	שִׁשָּׁה
seven	שֶׁבַע	שִׁבְעָה
eight	שְׁמֹנֶה	שְׁמֹנָה
nine	תִּשַׁע	תִּשְׁעָה
ten	עֶשֶׂר	עֲשָׂרָה

(see p. 73 for brief notes
on the Numerals)

English-Hebrew Vocabulary
(Only words found in the exercises are listed)

A
able, be יָכֹל
abundance רֹב, מְאֹד
add יָסַף
after אַחַר
age עַד, עוֹלָם
all כֹּל, כָּל־
also אַף
altar מִזְבֵּחַ
answer עָנָה
approach נָגַשׁ
army חַיִל
ashamed, be בּוֹשׁ
atone כָּפַר

B
bad רַע
battle מִלְחָמָה
be הָיָה
bear a child יָלַד
because לְמַעַן, כִּי
become הָיָה
befall קָרָא, קָרָה
begin חָלַל
behold! הֵן, הִנֵּה
beside עַל
between בֵּין
blood דָּם
book סֵפֶר
boundary גְּבוּל
bow down שָׁחָה
boy נַעַר
bread לֶחֶם
break in pieces שָׁבַר
breath רוּחַ

brother אָח
build בָּנָה
burn שָׂרַף
burnt offering עוֹלָה
bury קָבַר

C
call קָרָא
capture לָכַד
cast שָׁלַךְ
cattle בְּהֵמָה
cease שָׁבַת
chief רַב
cleave to דָּבַק
come to pass הָיָה
command צִוָּה
commandment מִצְוָה
complete, be כָּלָה
comprehend כּוּל
concerning עַל
consume אָכַל
contain כּוּל
count סָפַר
covenant בְּרִית
create בָּרָא
cross over עָבַר
cubit אַמָּה
cut, cut off כָּרַת

D
daughter בַּת
day יוֹם
death מָוֶת
declare נָגַד
deed מַעֲשֶׂה
deliver נָצַל, יָשַׁע

destroy שָׁמַד, שָׁחַת
die מוּת
discern בִּין
disposses יָרַשׁ
distress רַע
do עָשָׂה
do good יָטַב
draw near קָרַב
drink שָׁתָה
dwell יָשַׁב, שָׁכֵן

E
eat אָכַל
earth אֶרֶץ
elder, an זָקֵן
enter בּוֹא
eon עוֹלָם
establish כּוּן
eternity עוֹלָם
every כָּל־, כֹּל
evil, be רָעַע
exceedingly מְאֹד
eye עַיִן

F
face פָּנִים
fall נָפַל
father אָב
fear יָרֵא
field שָׂדֶה
fight לָחַם
finish כָּלָה
flock צֹאן
food לֶחֶם
fountain עַיִן
from מִן

G

garment בֶּגֶד
girl נַעֲרָה
give נָתַן
glory כָּבוֹד
go הָלַךְ
go about סָבַב
God אֱלֹהִים
go in בּוֹא
go down יָרַד
gold זָהָב
good, be יָטַב
good טוֹב
go out יָצָא
go to ruin שָׁחַת
go up עָלָה
grace חֵן
great גָּדוֹל
ground אֶרֶץ
guard שָׁמַר

H

hate שָׂנֵא
he who אֲשֶׁר
hear שָׁמַע
heart לֵבָב,לֵב
heavens שָׁמַיִם
heavy, be כָּבֵד
high, be רוּם
holiness קֹדֶשׁ
holy קָדֵשׁ
holy, be קָדֵשׁ
honor v. כָּבֵד n. כָּבוֹד
horse סוּס
house בַּיִת
how? אֵיכָה or אֵיךְ
how! same

I

if כִּי, אִם
incline נָטָה
in order that לְמַעַן
inquire of דָּרַשׁ
instead of תַּחַת
instruct יָרָה
instruction תּוֹרָה
integrity תָּם
I pray נָא-

J

judge שָׁפַט
judgment מִשְׁפָּט

K

kill מוּת, הָרַג
king מֶלֶךְ
kneel בָּרַךְ
know יָדַע

L

land אֲדָמָה, אֶרֶץ
law תּוֹרָה
lead הָלַךְ
leader אַיִל
learn לָמַד
lest פֶּן
life נֶפֶשׁ
lift up נָשָׂא
live חָיָה
lodge לִין,לוּן
LORD יְהֹוָה
loving kindness חֶסֶד

M

make עָשָׂה
make atonement כָּפַר
make known יָדַע
man אָדָם,אִישׁ

mankind אָדָם
many, be רָבָה,רָבַב
march הָלַךְ
meet קָרָא,קָרָה
mercy חֶסֶד
midst תָּוֶךְ, קֶרֶב
mind לֵבָב, לֵב
money כֶּסֶף
month חֹדֶשׁ
mother אֵם
mountain הַר
mouth פֶּה
much רַב
multiply רָבָה,רָבַב
multitude רֹב

N

name שֵׁם
nation גּוֹי
new moon חֹדֶשׁ
night לַיְלָה
not לֹא
now עַתָּה

O

old, be זָקֵן
old זָקֵן
offer קָרַב
offspring זֶרַע
on עַל
on account of יַעַן
only רַק

P

palm (of hand) כַּף
peace שָׁלוֹם
people עַם
person נֶפֶשׁ
pierce חָלַל

place n.מָקוֹם,v.שׂוּם	scattered,be פּוּץ	surround סָבַב
plague נֶגַע	sea יָם	sword חֶרֶב
please נָא	see רָאָה	**T**
pollute חָלַל	seed זֶרַע	teach לָמַד
possess יָרַשׁ	seek דָּרַשׁ, בָּקַשׁ	tent אֹהֶל
praise הָלַל	send,send away שָׁלַח	territory גְּבוּל
priest כֹּהֵן	servant עֶבֶד	that כִּי
prince שַׂר	serve עָבַד	then אָז
proclaim קָרָא	set נָתַן	there שָׁם
prophet נָבִיא	sheep צֹאן	therefore עַל־כֵּן
purify חָטָא	show favor חָנַן	there is יֵשׁ
pursue רָדַף	silver כֶּסֶף	these אֵלֶּה
put נָתַן, שׂוּם	sin חָטָא	this m.זֶה f.זֹאת
put on(clothes)לָבַשׁ	sit יָשַׁב	thither שָׁמָּה
R	sky שָׁמַיִם	thousand אֶלֶף
ram אַיִל	slay הָרַג	throw יָרָה, שָׁלַךְ
reach נָגַע	smite נָכָה	thus כֵּן
reign מָלַךְ	snatch נָצַל	time עֵת
remember זָכַר	so כֵּן	touch נָגַע
rest שָׁבַת	sojourn גּוּר	towards אֶל
return שׁוּב	sole(of foot)כַּף	transgress עָבַר
reverence יָרֵא	son בֵּן	travail חוּל
rich, be כָּבֵד	soul נֶפֶשׁ	tree עֵץ
ride רָכַב	sound קוֹל	tribe מַטֶּה, שֵׁבֶט
rise קוּם	speak דָּבַר	turn aside סוּר
rise early שָׁכַם	spirit רוּחַ	turn back שׁוּב
road דֶּרֶךְ	staff מַטֶּה, שֵׁבֶט	**U**
rod מַטֶּה, שֵׁבֶט	stand קוּם, עָמַד	under תַּחַת
round about סָבִיב	stone אֶבֶן	until עַד
rule מָשַׁל	strength חַיִל	unto אֶל
run רוּץ	stretch out נָטָה	**V**
S	strike נָגַע	visit פָּקַד
sacrifice n.זֶבַח v.זָבַח	stroke נֶגַע	voice קוֹל
sanctify קָדַשׁ	strong, be חָזַק	**W**
save יָשַׁע, חָיָה	stumble כָּשַׁל	war מִלְחָמָה
say אָמַר	surely רַק	way דֶּרֶךְ

welfare שָׁלוֹם	wife אִשָּׁה	write כָּתַב
what? מַה,מָה־	wind רוּחַ	writhe חוּל
wherefore? מַדּוּעַ	with עָמַד,עִם,אֵת	**Y**
which אֲשֶׁר	woman אִשָּׁה	yea אַף
whirl חוּל	wood עֵץ	year שָׁנָה
who? מִי	word דָּבָר	**Addenda**
who אֲשֶׁר	work מַעֲשֶׂה	afflict עָנָה
wicked רָשָׁע	worship שָׁחָה	before לִפְנֵי
		bless בָּרַךְ
		take לָקַח, לָכַד

Index